FIRST DOWN HOUSTON

THE BIRTH OF AN NFL FRANCHISE

FIRST DOWN

PHOTOGRAPHS BY ROBERT CLARK

ANNE WILKES TUCKER, WITH ESSAY BY MICKEY HERSKOWITZ

THE MUSEUM OF FINE ARTS, HOUSTON

THE BIRTH OF AN NFL FRANCHISE

HOUSTON

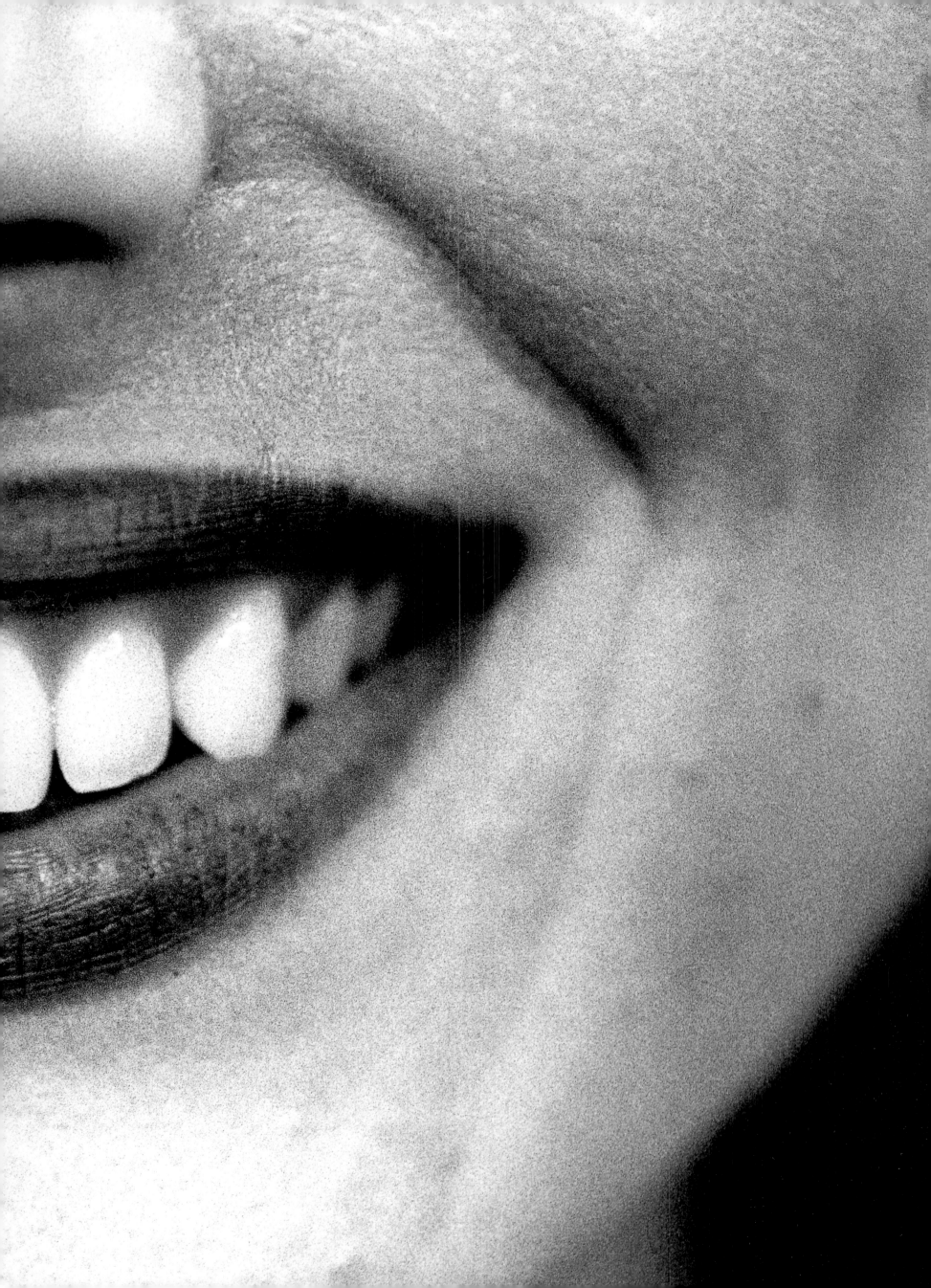

The exhibition *First Down Houston: The Birth of an NFL Franchise* has been co-organized by the
Museum of Fine Arts, Houston, and the Houston Texans.

Support for this exhibition is provided by **SIEMENS**, Janice S. and Robert C. McNair,
and the Houston Texans.

Exhibition Dates
The Museum of Fine Arts, Houston
September 21, 2003–February 8, 2004

Art Direction and Design by Erin Mayes and DJ Stout,
Pentagram Design, Austin, Texas

Book Typeset in Conduit and Iowan Old Style

Printed in Italy by Amilcare Pizzi, Milan

ISBN 0-89090-122-8

INTRODUCTION
BY JANICE AND ROBERT McNAIR

THE HOUSTON TEXANS' INAUGURAL SEASON WAS incredibly exciting and memorable! The birth of the Texans was witnessed by the world on national television with a level of excitement Houston has rarely seen. New names, new faces, in a world-class stadium—winning, losing, new challenges—all experiences that we treasure and will never forget.

Even before Texans Quarterback David Carr took his first snap, projects were under way to memorialize the first season and enhance our football stadium and community.

From August 30 through September 7, 2003, the first of these projects will be presented to the public during Texans week:

Bronze sculptures by Walter Matia symbolizing *the Spirit of the Bull— pride, courage, strength, tradition, independence* — will be unveiled at Reliant Stadium's entrance.

September 21, the other two projects will be introduced to the public.

A book, *First Down Houston: The Birth of an NFL Franchise,* with photography by Robert Clark, documents in unusual and insightful fashion the 2002 Texans' season. The 225 photographs provide a penetrating and intimate look into the world of our team.

An exhibition in conjunction with *First Down Houston* will be on view at the Museum of Fine Arts, Houston, from September 21, 2003, through February 8, 2004. It will, of course, be on view through Super Bowl XXXVIII.

The bringing together of sports and art is another example of how beauty can be found if we look for it. It also reflects the success of differing endeavors working together to produce projects that enhance the quality of life in our community.

The Museum of Fine Arts, Houston, the Glassell School of Art, the Cultural Arts Council of Houston/

JANICE AND BOB MCNAIR, 2002

Harris County, and the entire staff of the Texans have worked hard to make these projects possible. The director of the Museum of Fine Arts, Houston, Dr. Peter Marzio, has enthusiastically encouraged these efforts and lent invaluable artistic expertise. We are grateful for the interest and significance these projects give the Texans. Thank you all.

May we enjoy and remember our year 2002. Now, *Let's Roll!*

JANICE S. AND ROBERT C. McNAIR

AS THE OFFICIAL INTEGRATED BUILDING SOLUTIONS provider for Reliant Stadium, Siemens salutes the Houston Texans on their inaugural season. We are proud to be the corporate sponsor of *First Down Houston: The Birth of an NFL Franchise*, an exhibition of photography by Robert Clark at the Museum of Fine Arts, Houston.

SIEMENS

MORE THAN A GAME
BY MICKEY HERSKOWITZ

WE ALWAYS KNEW THAT RELIGION WAS IMPORTANT IN Texas, really big, because people kept comparing it to football.

Which recalls a time many years ago, when a writer postponed his wedding day so he could cover a high school football game in which Pflugerville – yes, Pflugerville – was gunning for a record of fifty straight victories.

"What I remember best about that game," he said, years later, "is that the preacher who gave the invocation prayed for a victory. He said, 'Lord, we got to have this one tonight.' Just said it flat out. I had never heard that before."

Somewhere along the way, we may have confused football with the Meaning of Life, which is surely understandable. But even in the pros the clergy are not licensed to pray for anything as coarse as winning. They are supposed to pray for a well-fought game, for the avoidance of injury, and for no gang fights in the parking lot.

I once interviewed a retired defensive back named Lester Hayes, who had starred as a Houston schoolboy, a Texas Aggie and an Oakland Raider. By the end of his playing days, his most cherished pieces of jewelry were a gold crucifix he wore around his neck, and his two Super Bowl rings. The one from Super Bowl XV, a win over the Philadelphia Eagles, was locked in a safe. The other, earned three years later, had been auctioned off on the Internet for $18,200. It had languished in a Reno pawnshop for nearly a year.

Please do not jump to the nearest conclusion. This is neither a tale of hearts and flowers nor one of a busted ex-jock who was down and out. This is the condensed version of what happened:

Hayes was in Reno for a sports memorabilia show. Had an abscess in his mouth "the size of a walnut." Found a dental clinic. When asked how he would pay, he reached for his billfold and found an empty back pocket (his wallet was in a pair of trousers at home).

When you are hurting with an abscessed tooth that feels as if it had invaded your right eye, you do not think with absolute clarity. He needed eight hundred dollars and he found it in a pawn shop. He removed the ring and kept the cross because "I couldn't take out a loan on Jesus."

He had four months, plenty of time to reclaim it, but a prostate problem clobbered him. He spent most of 1999 in bed and in pain. The pawnbroker gave him a final notice and when he didn't pick up the ring, it went to the highest bidder on eBay. Lester isn't dumb, just afflicted, as many in the perspiring arts are, with a sweet irresponsibility.

The last I heard, he was still trying to trace the anonymous purchaser and buy back a ring he could have recovered for the price of the loan, plus $320 in interest.

But the point is, he could have covered his dental bill by hocking the gold cross, but he did not. Which reminds us that football, at any level, has a spiritual and mental and emotional side that is beyond, well, beyond Pflugerville.

You can walk into any locker room before a game and feel the intensity, the edginess, the tension. Some players can't tell you the name of the guy who lines up next to them. But whatever trance they are in, to whatever lengths they are prepared to go, all of it is in pursuit of that elusive piece of jewelry, which is what makes Lester's story funny and poignant and painful at the same time.

Today Hayes is rooting for the Houston Texans, partly because they are now the hometown team, and partly because, as an expansion franchise, a year old, they are the classic underdogs. And Texas is the holy temple of heroic defeats, or have we forgotten the Alamo?

Hayes was a terrific and colorful player for the Raiders, one who had at least a minor role in a decision by the NFL to outlaw a substance called "stickum," a caramel-colored adhesive widely used for a time by both receivers and defensive backs. They practically dipped their arms in the stuff.

When the league banned it, Hayes was asked what effect he thought the new legislation would have. "You won't see guys catching passes with their elbows anymore," he replied.

POETS AND SCHOLARS HAVE LONG ATTEMPTED TO explain why the game gets such a grip on our hearts and throats. So what is this fatal attraction called football? To begin with, every autumn it carries us back to our youth; no, not our childhood, but our swinging youth, when we had all the answers, never mind the questions. Football is more than what the players do.

Among other things, football is a social event and sometimes it is mass hysteria; it's nostalgia and waiting for next year and a clash of cultures:

It is the poetess Marianne Moore, remembering a student she had in a commercial law course she taught at the Carlisle Indian School, in Pennsylvania. His name was Jim Thorpe, a pureblood member of the Sac and Fox, as great a football player who ever lived and a one-man track team. Miss Moore saw him compete, but that wasn't how she remembered him. "He was a gentleman," she said. "I called him James. It would have seemed condescending, I thought, to call him Jim."

Football is Francis Schmidt, who coached great teams at Texas Christian University, before he coached greater teams at Ohio State. He was an absent-minded professor type, whose preoccupation with the game was legendary. Schmidt drove his car into a filling station in Columbus to have the oil changed. He stayed behind the wheel, drawing plays in a notebook, while the car was raised on a hoist.

Oblivious to the world around him, the coach pored over his diagrams. In a few minutes, he came up with a play that looked unstoppable.

With a small cry of triumph, Schmidt slapped the notebook shut, opened the car door, stepped out – and fell ten feet to the pavement. (Somehow, he was not seriously hurt and the play worked.)

Football is Broadway Joe Namath "guaranteeing" victory for his New York Jets over the mighty, 19-point-favorite Baltimore Colts in the third Circus Maximus. It's Weeb Ewbank, the Jets' kindly, pudgy coach, flanked by Namath and watching the final seconds wind down in that historic win over his former team. In a spooky, if touching, flashback, Ewbank called out across the field to quarterback Johnny Unitas, whom he had coached a decade earlier, "No interceptions now, John."

It's the obnoxious guy behind you who is always rooting for the wrong team. It's singing the fight song after the other team has just gone ahead by five touchdowns. It's the high school cheerleader with the upswept hairdo, when you're a sophomore and she's a senior, the most unattainable woman in any guy's life.

Football is Tad Jones, of Yale, telling his players: "Gentlemen, you are about to play Harvard. Nothing you do in life will ever again be so important as what you do on that field today."

Football is fear. It's Leomont Evans suffering a spinal cord bruise, the injury every player dreads, in the Hall of Fame game, in Canton, Ohio, in the Texans' national debut. Through the mist of his medication, Evans, a fifth-year defensive back from Clemson, found the owner of the team at his bedside. Bob McNair took his hand, kneeled and prayed with him. Evans' season, after a few minutes in a preseason game, had ended, as had perhaps his career, but the news that mattered was good: he would recover.

Football is all about loyalty, and not knowing what kind of crisis will launch an 11-game winning streak. The Oilers were 1-and-4 in 1993 and playing on the road, in New England, when David Williams, an offensive tackle, chose to stay home and watch his wife give birth instead of joining his team. No one could have predicted the controversy that would follow the birth of Scot Williams, the most famous infant since Baby Jane or even Baby Snooks. When ex-quarterback Gifford Nielsen asked Bum Phillips about it on his weekly TV show, the former Oilers coach tried to be diplomatic. "Well, hell," he said, "I don't know what he was doing there (in the delivery room) in the first place. When it gets to that point, the daddy has done his job." Responded Nielsen: "We'll be back after this commercial."

Football was never meant to be life or death, we keep saying, but you had to make an occasional exception for the Oilers. For the die-hard fan, the game is only slightly more essential than air.

It's Franco Harris and the Immaculate Reception, the Texas Special, Luv Ya Blue, the Notre Dame Victory March and Brian's Song. It's Darrell Royal, asking his Longhorns to play each week "as if they were planting the flag on Iwo Jima."

Football is a writer paraphrasing Rudyard Kipling, in the heyday of the now deceased Southwest Conference: "The temper of friends, the lover of your life, or the favored conference member; which of the three will survive the strife of a frenzied Texas November?"

It's the Jack-o'-Lantern smile of Vince Lombardi and the hound's-tooth check hat of Bear Bryant and Tom Landry, with that Dick Tracy jaw and proper hat with the brim just right. It's Bill Petersen, who had a tendency to mangle the language, scolding his Houston Oilers for their casual reaction to the National Anthem. "I want you to stand on your helmets," he ordered, "with the sideline under your arm." Poor Pete, who had success at Florida State and Rice, was fired after his Oiler teams won once in 18 games.

Football is the glory that was Roman Gabriel and the grandeur that was Bob Griese; not to overlook the exquisite timing of Joe Montana, John Elway and Dan Marino, racing the clock, bringing their teams from behind.

It's the immortal Bobby Layne, beating a driving-while-intoxicated rap in Detroit after his lawyer argued that the arresting officer mistook his Texas drawl for a drunken slur. And finding a banner over the door of the Lions' locker room that read: "AH ALL AIN'T DRUNK. AH ALL AM FROM TEXAS."

Football is all those wonderful nicknames: The Gipper, Choo Choo Charlie Justice, Crazy Legs Hirsch, Big Daddy Lipscomb, Night Train Lane, Too Tall Jones, Mr. Inside and Mr. Outside, Glenn Davis and Doc Blanchard, Slingin' Sammy Baugh, Whizzer White, Squirmin' Herman Wedemeyer (who later played a cop on the TV series, *Hawaii Five-O.*). The true fan chokes up at the thought that someone would cheer, "Fight fiercely, Harvard."

Football is a sign lettered in script on the lawn of a church in Fayetteville, Arkansas, on a Saturday afternoon in the fall: "Material Things Are Transient. Spiritual Things Last Forever. Nevertheless, Beat Texas."

Football is Earl Campbell, running so hard that one coach asked the officials to check his thigh pads for metal plates after the game. And here was Earl, who could carry on an entire conversation by quoting country music lyrics, announcing his retirement: "It's like that Merle Haggard song, the only thing I got to worry about now is the rest of my life. But I won't worry about it long. Like Willie Nelson says, 'Cowboys are special with their own brand of miseries.' "

Football is the 41st president, George Herbert Walker Bush, returning to Washington on the Texans' team plane to watch them lose to the Redskins. The Texans' encounter marked only the second time Charley Casserly had been back to FedEx Field, since new owner Dan Snyder fired him as general manager in 1999. The night before the game, he was a houseguest of former owner John Kent Cooke.

This, too, is football: a 27-or 28-year-old Casserly working one year for George Allen without pay because he knew this was where he wanted to be. "One night I woke up in a cold sweat," he says. "I thought, 'My God, I'm sleeping on a Goodwill mattress on the floor and I've got $500 in the bank and I'm driving a car with 120,000 miles on it with a driver's side door that won't open and now I'm taking a job that pays nothing. What have I done?' "

Football is Grantland Rice, in his overcoat, hunched over a portable typewriter, pecking out his unforgettable lead: "Outlined against a blue-gray October sky, the four horsemen rode again." And in the minute or so it took to type the words, the Notre Dame backfield of Jim Crowley, Harry Stuhldreher, Elmer Layden and Don Miller became the most famous in football lore.

It's the Rams' Fearsome Foursome, Minnesota's Purple People Eaters, Texas A&M's Junction Boys, Washington's Over-the-Hill Gang and Miami's No-Name Defense.

Football is Roger Staubach describing heaven as a place "where quarterbacks complete all their passes." Asked what the defensive backs would be doing while this was going on, Roger replied, "There are no defensive backs in heaven."

It's trying to decide which linebacker was the toughest or meanest, Dick Butkus or Ray Nitschke or Lawrence Taylor or Joe Schmidt or Sam Huff. And you know who would receive Vince Lombardi's vote. When a coaching tower toppled over and landed on one of his players, Vince was the first to reach the flattened figure. Then he waved everyone back. "It's okay," he said, "it's Nitschke."

Football is a game for our times, the times being violent, as times usually are. But it is also a game of grace and glory and grit. It's Lou Rymkus coaching the Houston Oilers to the first championship the American Football League ever awarded, and getting fired a year later.

It's the game within the game—high finance and occasional low comedy. Three times the National Football League tried to slip an expansion team back into Los Angeles, but no one stepped up, not with hard cash or a stadium plan. And Bob McNair, who simply wouldn't accept the odds against Houston, made a wipeout offer and dazzled the expansion committee with a model of a 69,000-seat palace with a retractable roof. This would become Reliant Stadium.

McNair, who made his fortune by founding his own energy company, did the seemingly impossible. He blended the past to the future and made it work, calling the new team the Texans, a name that had been attached to at least four teams that failed. For the $700 million that McNair and his partners paid for the NFL's 32nd franchise, he could have called them the Chicken Fried Steaks, if he wished, a tribute to Houston's traditional cuisine. He was entitled to call them whatever he wanted.

But, to the surprise of many, the name is wearing well, and on the plus side the name is not one any other state is likely to steal. It clearly has a certain historical charm, having been abandoned by teams in Dallas twice, in Houston and even San Antonio, whose teams briefly competed in the Canadian League. We do not count minor league hockey or soccer teams.

We have discovered that if you ignore history, you are only doomed to repeat it until you get it right.

Few will remember the original Dallas Texans, which isn't entirely a bad thing. They were formerly the New York Football Yankees, and based in Boston before that, having been owned by Ted Collins, the manager of singer Kate Smith.

In 1952, the team was moved to Dallas, where the new owners were the Miller brothers, heirs to a textile fortune. But they were unprepared to lose their shirts. At midseason, they gave back the franchise, and the club finished on the road. This was not a team bereft of talent. The roster included Buddy Young, an exciting little runner, and future Hall of Famers in Gino Marchetti at end and Art Donovan at tackle. For the season's final five weeks, the team practiced in Hershey, Pennsylvania, taking the position that everybody had to be somewhere. This was an exercise in running out the clock. Most of their time was spent playing volleyball over the goal posts.

Those Texans were a mixed bag of styles and temper. They obtained Forrest (Chubby) Grigg for ex-Browns, ex-Rice great Weldon Humble. In Young's words, Grigg was "mean as a snake, fat as a hog, on the downside of his career."

The Lost Battalion went on to become the Baltimore Colts, eventually landing in Indianapolis.

Lamar Hunt, the founder of the American Football League, revived the name—what sentimental fools we

mortals be–in 1960. The new Dallas Texans slugged it out with the Cowboys for three years, then folded their tents and slipped away to Kansas City. They re-emerged as the Chiefs and lost to Green Bay in the first Super Bowl game, in January of 1967.

As a member of the ill-fated World Football League, the Houston Texans left us with one hilarious memory. They persuaded a goofy giant named John Matuszak, a first-round draft pick by the Oilers, to switch leagues early in the 1974 season. His teammates thought it was suspicious when The Tooz took his helmet, pads and shoes home with him. The next night he suited up for the Texans, his helmet having been spray-painted with the colors of his new team.

He was removed from the field after being served with a court order, making judicial history on the spot. The case wound up in court, where he lost a suit against the Oilers, the NFL, his former agent and others. When the Texans moved to Shreveport, they did not go unwept. They had plenty of creditors, including their lawyers. You can afford to sue lots of people if you don't pay your lawyers.

Matuszak, who would go on to greater celebrity with the Raiders, testified that he passed up an offer to play in Canada, staying in the USA even though he hated the NFL. "I love my country," he said, adding in a touching afterthought, "The home of the free and the land of the brave."

The legacy might have troubled a lesser organization, but the newest and now genuine Texans were equal to the task. McNair, general manager Charley Casserly and Coach Dom Capers assembled a team that delivered mightily on opening night, leaving the Dallas Cowboys stunned and mortified in a 19-10 upset. David Carr, their first pick in the draft, their franchise quarterback, connected with Corey Bradford on a 65-yard touchdown pass to break a 10-10 tie in the fourth quarter.

So, yes, football is having a sense of history and a sense of humor. There wasn't the usual weirdness associated with expansion teams, except when Houston trounced Pittsburgh on the road, 24-6. The Texans offense completed three passes and gained a total of 47 yards, the lowest total by a winning team in NFL history. Meanwhile, the defense scored three touchdowns, two by Aaron Glenn, who returned interceptions for 70 and 65 yards. Some were tempted to see the win as payback for the Oilers' bitter losses to a Steeler dynasty in the late 1970s. The Oilers would take teams on the brink of greatness, and leave their blood, sweat and teeth on the turf at Three Rivers Stadium. Aaron Glenn, a product of Nimitz High in Humble, and Texas A&M University, will have none of it. "I grew up an Oilers fan," he says, "but this whole thing about the Oilers and the Texans, that's over. The past is dead and gone. If people want to see Pittsburgh lose, for whatever reason, fine. But we're the Texans. This is a whole new era. We have to make our own mark."

THE TEXANS WENT ON TO WIN FOUR GAMES, TYING THE second best production by an expansion team. The Carolina Panthers, under Capers, had seven wins and, in their second year came within a game of the Super Bowl, as did Jacksonville, the other newcomer. It was a Cinderella story so touching that the owners swore they would never again allow a new team to assemble that much talent.

But the measure of their debut season was whether the team improved each week, and the Texans, by most accounts, met that goal. Bob McNair, who was an original Oilers' ticket holder, who used to ride to the games on the private bus of his neighbor, Bud Adams, now had his own high-tech stadium, with Adams as a ticket holder.

Football, in Houston, in 2002, was an upstart team beating four foes who had a head start of at least 43 years.

TO ME, THIS IS THE ONE THING THAT MAKES PEOPLE GO IN THIS BUSINESS. EVERYTHING THAT YOU DO FOR AN ENTIRE WEEK LEADS UP TO THOSE THREE HOURS.

—DOM CAPERS, THE DAY BEFORE THE DALLAS GAME. OPENING NIGHT: THE HOUSTON TEXANS' INAUGURAL GAME. 2002

There are a lot of players from around this area. That's one thing the Texans are going to have in their favor—there are guys that are going to want to come here (to play.)
—STEVE MCKINNEY. OPENING NIGHT: THE HOUSTON TEXANS' INAUGURAL GAME. 2002

I'm very, very excited about everything that's going to happen Sept. 6. It's been in the works for months, and a lot of effort has gone into making it such a special occasion. We want to do it up right because we can only do it once. When we announce the nickname and unveil the logo and colors, we'll finally have an identity. We'll no longer be the Houston Whatchamacallits.
—ROBERT MCNAIR. "SET FOR UNVEILING BIG AS TEXAS." HOUSTON CHRONICLE, AUGUST 23, 2000

ANYONE WHO BUILDS A MANSION OF A FACILITY LIKE THE ONE HE'S (MCNAIR) BUILDING, YOU KNOW HE'S GOING TO DO EVERYTHING HE CAN TO MAKE THE TEAM A WINNER. AS A PLAYER, THAT'S ALL YOU CAN ASK FOR. IF YOU'RE GOING TO GIVE THEM EVERYTHING YOU'VE GOT ON THE FIELD, YOU WANT TO KNOW THEY'RE GOING TO BE TRYING JUST AS HARD OFF THE FIELD TO MAKE THIS TEAM A WINNER. WHEN I LOOK AT THOSE FACILITIES, I KNOW THIS ORGANIZATION IS ABOUT WINNING.

—DEFENSIVE TACKLE GARY WALKER ABOUT THE PRACTICE FACILITIES. HOUSTON CHRONICLE, MARCH 12, 2003

TEXAS FOOT

THIS IS ESP
I'VE BEEN TOLD
ANY OTHER
FORTY-

—ROBERT DRAPER. "WHAT DREAMS MAY COME." GQ, JULY 20

Surround yourself with good people, wor hard and have a plan.
—DOM CAPERS REMEMBERING AN IMPORTANT LESSON LEARNED FROM HIS FATHER. "TEXANS JUST RIGHT FOR CAPERS." HOUSTON CHRONICLE, JANUARY 22, 2001

Bob's such a class act and Houston's a great football town.
—EXPANSION COMMITTEE CO-CHAIR BOB KRAFT, OWNER OF THE NEW ENGLAND PATRIOTS. "IT'S TOUCHDOWN . . . . HOUSTON." HOUSTON CHRONICLE, OCTOBER 7, 1999

I HADN'T THROWN THE BALL THIS MUCH IN A WHILE
I'VE TRIED TO THROW THE BALL TO
MY DAD AND MY BROTHER
BUT THEY'RE NOT AS FAST AS JABAR GAFFNEY
SO THAT KIND OF THREW
OFF MY TIMING A LITTLE
I'M GOING TO HAVE TO GET USED TO THAT

—TEXANS QUARTERBACK DAVID CARR ON HIS FIRST DAY OF MINICAMP. HOUSTON CHRONICLE, APRIL 27, 2002

IS FOOTBALL AND BALL IS TEXAS. ECIALLY SO IN HOUSTON, WHICH NOT ONLY PRODUCES MORE NFL PLAYERS THAN CITY, BUT MORE PLAYERS THAN FOUR OTHER STATES.

HIS IS SOMETHING QUITE EXTRAORDINARY. IT'S NOT JUST HE RESURRECTION OF THE NFL IN HOUSTON BUT THE MAN- NER IN WHICH IT WAS DONE. TO COME BACK UNDER THESE CIR- CUMSTANCES IS VERY SPECIAL.

NFL COMMISSIONER PAUL TAGLIABUE ON COMING BACK TO HOUSTON. JUSTON CHRONICLE, MAY 14, 2002

When Dom came in, he had all of his notes in hand – his offensive plan, his defensive plan, how he organized his training camp. He had all his informa- tion in place, and he knew exactly what he wanted to do. It was quite clear that he had a vision, and he knew exactly what he wanted to accomplish and how he wanted to go about doing it. He was very impressive. —ROBERT MCNAIR. "CAPERS TAPPED AS TOP TEXANS." HOUSTON CHRONICLE, JANUARY 20, 2001

LET ME TELL YOU HOW I FEEL ABOUT BOB. I WOULD HAVE CARRIED HIM PIGGY BACK ACROSS THE DESERT TO HAVE HIM AS A PARTNER. —DALLAS COWBOYS OWNER JERRY JONES, WHO LOBBIED HARD TO GET THE EXPANSION FRANCHISE FOR HOUSTON. "ARE YOU READY FOR SOME FOOTBALL? OWNERS GLAD TO HAVE MCNAIR IN THEIR EXCLUSIVE CLUB." HOUSTON CHRONICLE, OCTOBER 7, 1999

wouldn't trade job for any job world because really to believe – now – we're become championship organization our can be proud of. CHARLEY CASSERLY. UILDING AN NFL TEAM ROM THE GROUND UP." JUSTON CHRONICLE, LY 30, 2000

IT'S KIND OF BAD WHEN WE'RE ALL LEARNING THROUGH THE MIDDLE OF THE FOOTBALL GAME. WE LEARN ON EACH PLAY, SO SOMETIMES IT CAN BE PRETTY UGLY, BUT OTHER TIMES WE LOOK ALL RIGHT. —ROOKIE QUARTERBACK DAVID CARR. "FIRST MEETING OF HOUSTON, EX-OILERS MORE BUSINESS THAN RIVALRY." DALLAS MORNING NEWS, NOVEMBER 10, 2002

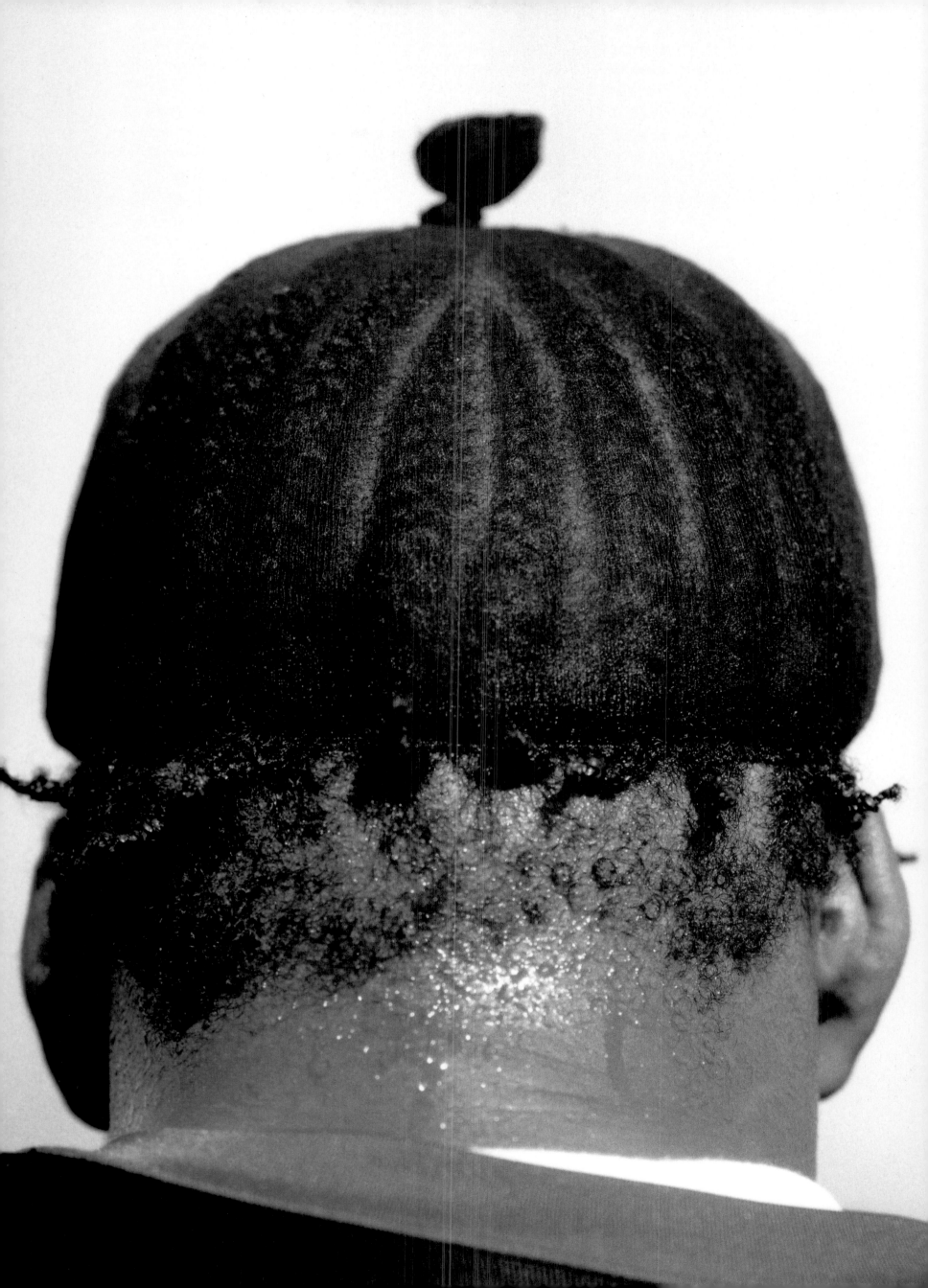

I try to keep it pretty loose leading up to a game. I don't try to get too geeked up. I just take the attitude that I'm going to have great practices all week. And as long as I practice well and don't commit mental errors, I feel very comfortable going into the game. I don't get nervous….. I've always believed that how you play on Sunday has already been determined by how you've practiced the week before.
— STEVE McKINNEY. OPENING NIGHT: THE HOUSTON TEXANS' INAUGURAL GAME. 2002

I'M READY TO PLAY WHEREVER YOU NEED ME TO PLAY. IT SHOULDN'T BE TOO TOUGH. PLAYING TACKLE YOU'RE OUT IN MORE SPACE. I JUST HAVE TO GET MY NECK A LITTLE STRONGER FOR THE BIG BOYS INSIDE, BUT I'M READY TO GO.
—OFFENSIVE LINE CHESTER PITTS. *HOUSTON CHRONICLE*, APRIL 21, 2002

RELIGIOUS FAITH IS SOMETHING I LIVE WITH BUT CAN'T REALLY EXPLAIN SOMETHING I BELIEVE NOBODY CAN TRULY EXPLAIN BUT I DON'T KNOW HOW I COULD PLAY THIS GAME WITHOUT IT

— DAVID CARR. "WHAT DRIVES DAVID CARR." *SPORTS ILLUSTRATED*, JANUARY–FEBRUARY 2003

CHARACTER IS A VERY IMPORTANT ISSUE. SOCIETY HAS CHANGED, AND PLAYERS ARE DIFFERENT. IT'S CRUCIAL THAT WE SPEND A LOT OF TIME AND EFFORT LOOKING INTO THEIR BACK GROUNDS TO MAKE SURE THEY FIT INTO OUR ORGANIZATION

— ROBERT MCNAIR. "BUILDING AN NFL TEAM FROM THE GROUND UP." *HOUSTON CHRONICLE*, JULY 30, 2000

MY TAPE HAS TO BE JUST RIGHT. WHEN I TAPE MY WRISTS, IT HAS TO BE THE SAME LENGTH ON BOTH ARMS. IF NOT, WE HAVE TO CUT IT OFF AND START OVER. BUT JON ISHOP KNOWS THAT. AND KEVIN BASTIN KNOWS HOW FAR DOWN TO TAPE MY ANKLES.

—AARON GLENN. OPENING NIGHT: THE HOUSTON TEXANS' INAUGURAL GAME. 2002

[The Dallas game] probably will be the biggest game I've ever played in. Being from Houston and knowing what the Houston-Dallas rivalry means to people in this state, I've already talked to a lot of people who are pumped up. Being about to play that game on Sunday night with the world watching is going to be great. I'm always up for prime time, but with it being our first game, and playing the Cowboys, it's going to be extra special. We want to win every game we play, but I'm sure the fans really want us to win those two games.

—CORNERBACK AARON GLENN, WHOSE INTERCEPTION IN THE SECOND QUARTER SET UP A 42-YARD FIELD GOAL, EXTENDING THE TEXANS LEAD TO 10-0 AGAINST THE DALLAS COWBOYS, QUOTED MARCH 27, 2002, HOUSTON CHRONICLE.

If you prepare, then you can take pressure and really work it to your advantage because you're more focused, you're more motivated and you're more disciplined.
— DOM CAPERS. OPENING NIGHT: THE HOUSTON TEXANS' INAUGURAL GAME. 2002

IN ADDITION TO ITS FOUR TEAM DOCTORS, THE TEAM ALSO EMPLOYS FOUR PARAMEDICS, TWO X-RAY TECHNICIANS, AN EYE DOCTOR, A DENTIST AND A CHIROPRACTOR ON GAME DAY.

ARTER TOOLE. OPENING NIGHT: THE HOUSTON TEXANS' INAUGURAL GAME. 2002

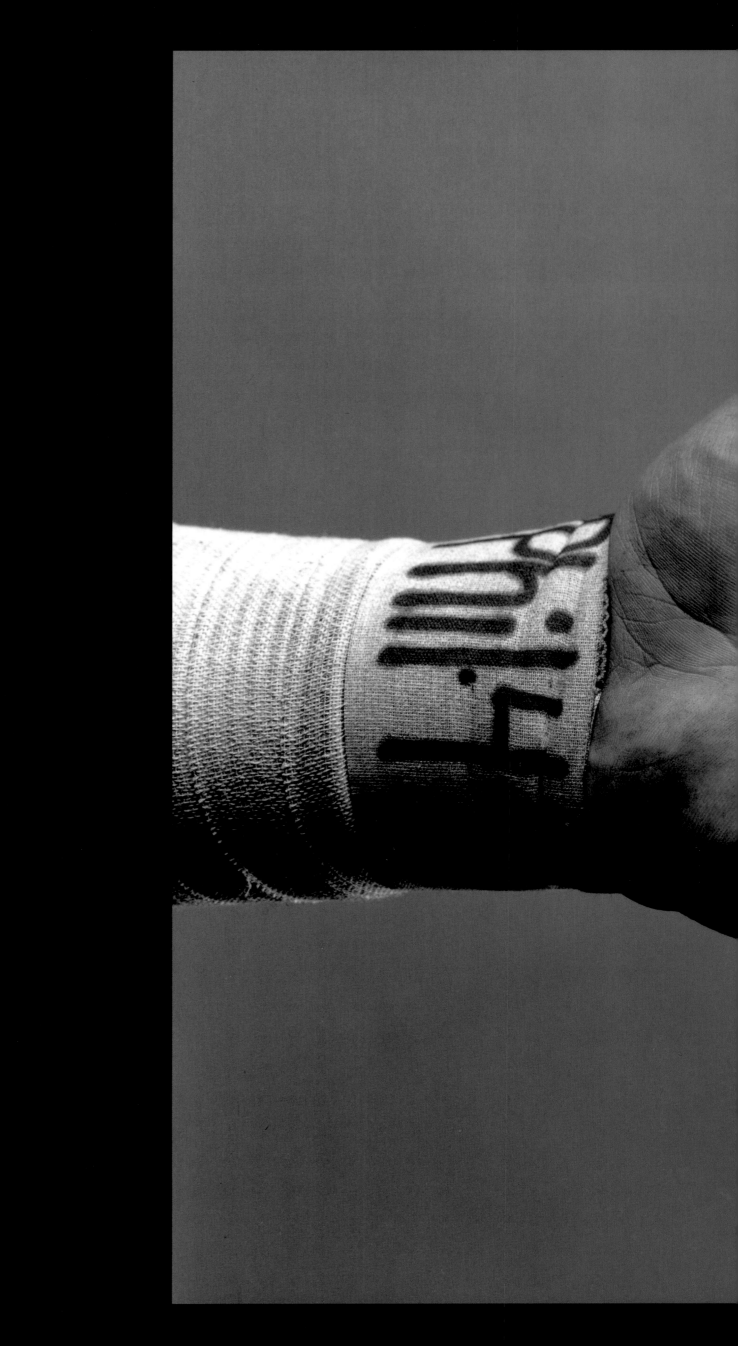

BILLY MILLER TIGHT END

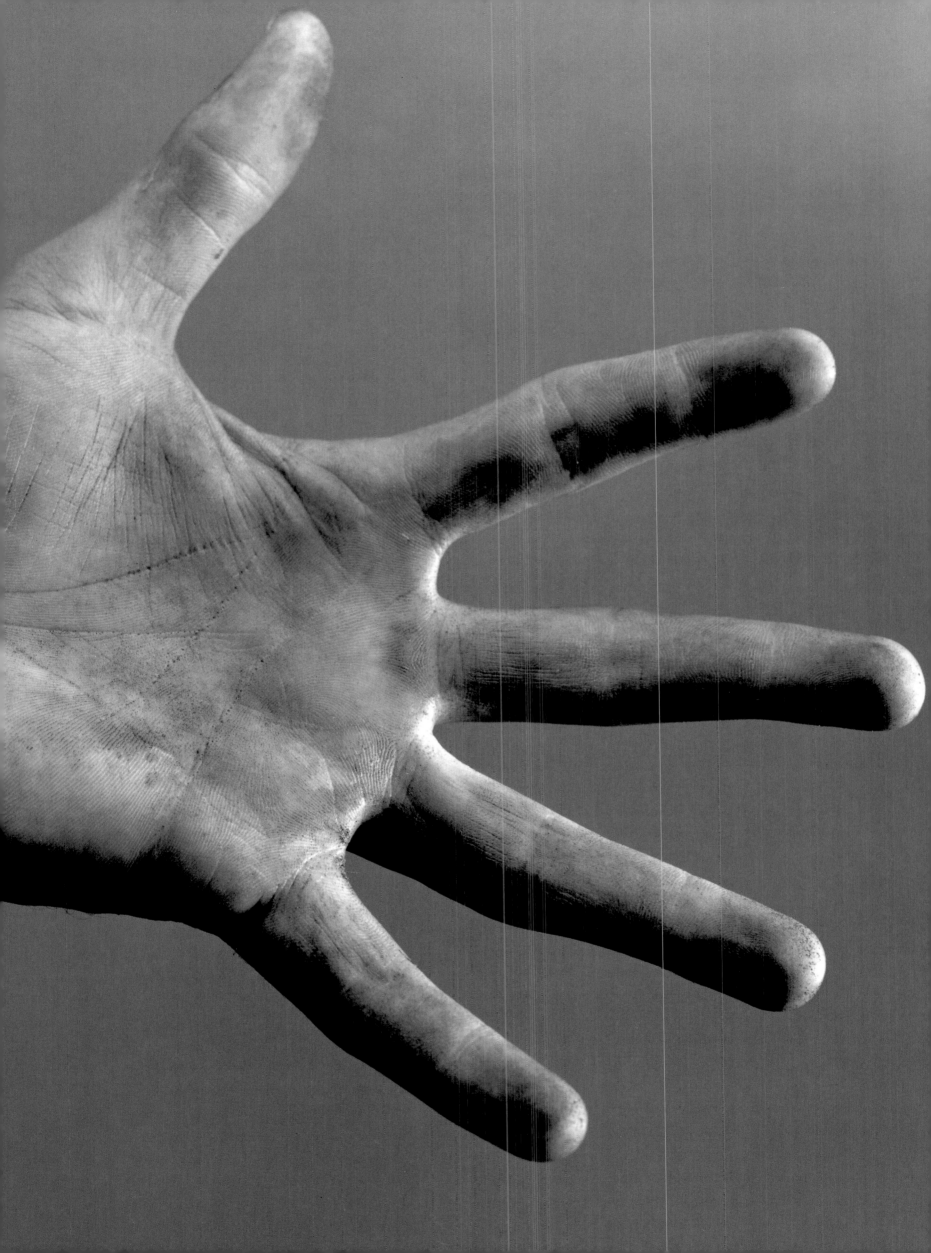

GARY WALKER DEFENSIVE TACKLE

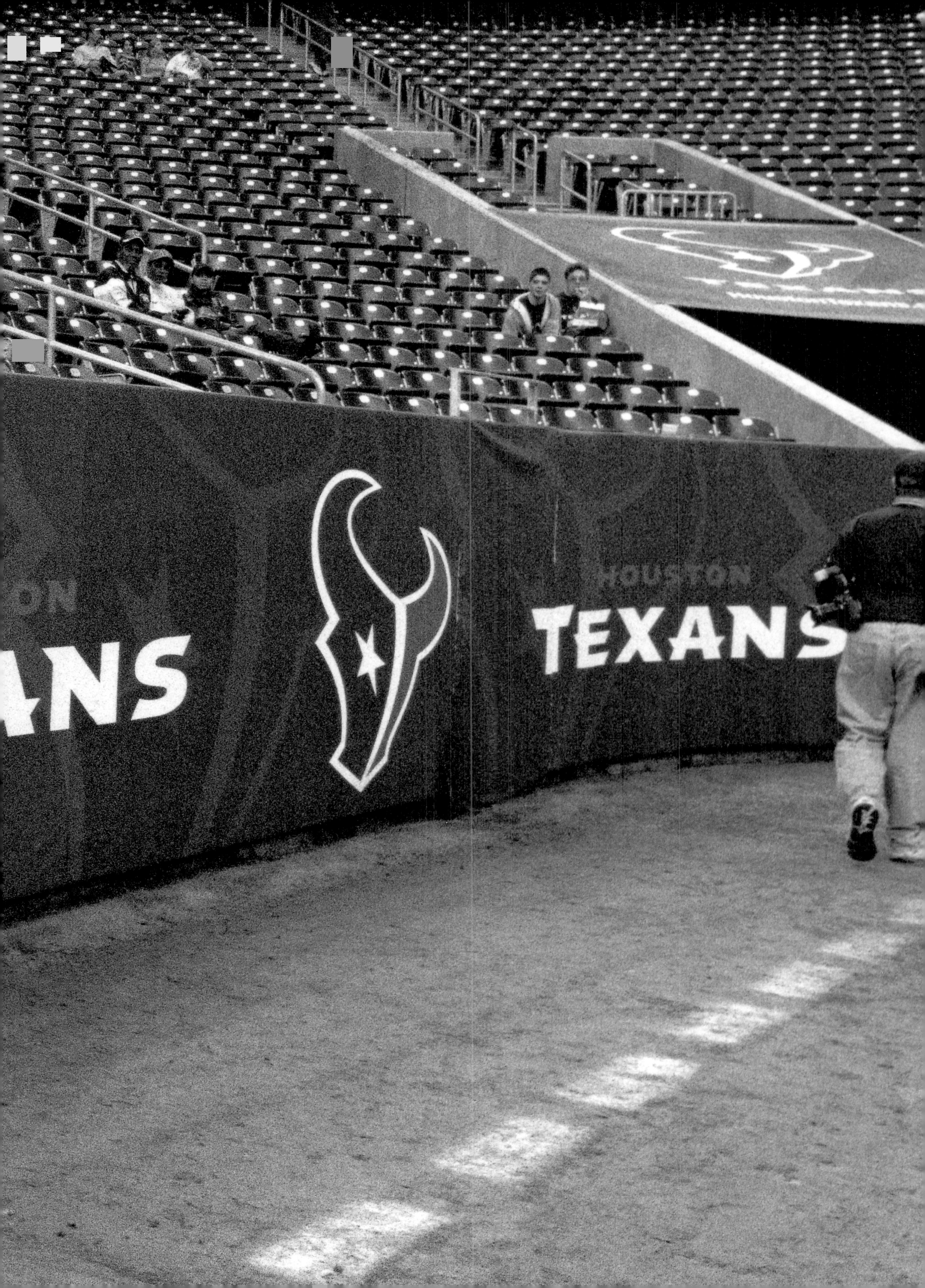

ANS
HOUSTON
TEXANS

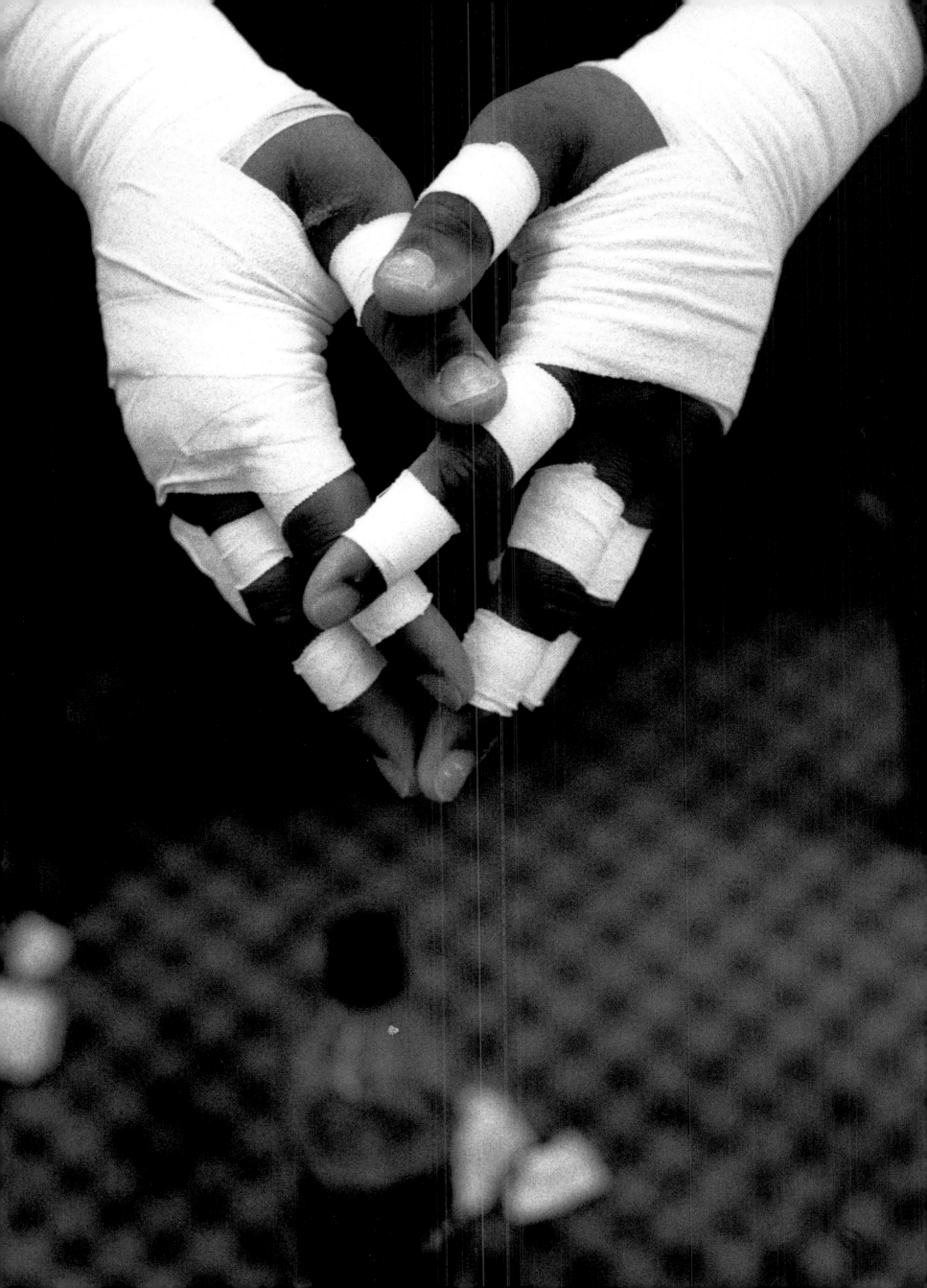

I CAN'T STAND THE COWBOYS.

I'VE BEEN A MAN WITHOUT A A COUNTRY FOR YEARS

[SINCE THE OILERS LEFT IN 1996].

—WAYNE CURTIS. "FOOTBALL FEAST." *HOUSTON CHRONICLE*, SEPTEMBER 2002

PASS PROTECTION IS ALL ABOUT PRIDE. I LOVE DAVID'S TOUGHNESS, BUT I'D RATHER BE TALKING TO YOU ABOUT HOW ACCURATE HIS PASSES ARE INSTEAD OF HOW TOUGH HE IS.

—JAMES ALLEN REGARDING THE NUMBER OF SACKS DAVID CARR SUFFERED. "REALITY CHECK." *HOUSTON CHRONICLE*, SEPTEMBER 16, 2002

Chester Pitts did not play football i high school; he wa a track man. The reason is the scho he attended did not have a footbal program. He was walk-on that tried out for the footba team at San Dieg State and ended up starting the las year and a half.

—GIL BRANDT ON SECON ROUND DRAFT CHOICE, 6 320 LBS, OFFENSIVE TAC CHESTER PITTS. NFL.CO APRIL 21, 2002

I've been coach of the year twice. I've been head coach of a Pro Bowl team. But you have a sense of not being fulfilled until you and win the Super Bowl. Obviously, from Day 1 here, that's your goal, and everything you do has to be geared toward that. And y have to have a plan—a blueprint—that will enable you to do that

—HEAD COACH DOM CAPERS ON DEVELOPING THE TEXANS. *SAN ANTONIO EXPRESS-NEWS*, APRIL 17, 2002

'M NERVOUS. BEFORE EVERY GAME
'M NERVOUS. BUT WHEN YOU GET
OUT THERE, THE ADRENALINE TAKES
OVER. THE FANS WANT TO JUST
REACH OUT AND TOUCH YOU. THEY
GRAB YOUR POM AND GIVE YOU A
HIGH FIVE. IT MAKES YOU FEEL JUST
AS SPECIAL AS THE FOOTBALL TEAM.

—REGINA, CHEERLEADER. "NO ORDINARY ROUTINE."
HOUSTON CHRONICLE, NOVEMBER 25, 2002

They say they are: intelligent. Self-assured. Married. Professional. Mothers. Daughters. Single. Blond. Brunette. Black. White. Asian. Hispanic. Educated. Most of all, they are ready. Ready to take their place as Houston Texans Cheerleaders.

Ever since Carr's high school days, he has carried laminated scripture— Jeremiah 29:11 and the Psalms are his favorites— under the insole of his right shoe, along with a cross. Asked if he does this even when he plays, he replies, "Especially when I play."

—"WHAT DRIVES DAVID CARR." *SPORTS ILLUSTRATED*, JANUARY-FEBRUARY 2003

THIS I
WE LOVE OU
WE
OUR C

ERICA, 28, A TEXANS CHEERLEADER AND NATIVE HOUSTONIAN. "BOOT-SCOOTIN BEA

HAVE A CERTAIN WAY OF TAPING THAT
HE GUYS ARE ACCUSTOMED TO. I
LWAYS RIP THAT FIRST PIECE OF TAPE
FF SINCE IT HAS A FRAYED EDGE.
LAYERS CAN BE SUPERSTITIOUS. IF I
ORGET TO RIP OFF THAT INITIAL PIECE,
HEY'LL REMIND ME IMMEDIATELY.

KEVIN BASTIN, HEAD ATHLETIC TRAINER. OPENING NIGHT: THE HOUSTON TEXANS' INAUGURAL GAME. 2002

When the Texans brought me for a visit, I liked the facilities, and I liked the organization. They just made me feel welcome. When I went home and sat down with my family and friends, we started going over things that had happened the last couple of years in Green Bay and what my future would be like if I came here. We laid all the different scenarios on the table and the best scenario was coming here.
—COREY BRADFORD ON COMING TO THE TEXANS AS A UFA. *HOUSTON CHRONICLE*, MARCH 11, 2002

DOM CAPERS HAS A QUIETNESS ABOUT HIM, AND SOMETIMES HIS TWO STRONGEST TRAITS WON'T JUMP OUT AT YOU. BUT IF YOU GET TO KNOW HIM, YOU'LL FIND OUT THAT HE'S HIGHLY COMPETITIVE AND THAT HE LEAVES NO STONE UNTURNED.
—KEVIN STEELE, HEAD COACH AT BAYLOR. "READY AND STEADY." *HOUSTON CHRONICLE*, JANUARY 21, 2001

THE SOUTH.
R BEAUTY QUEENS, AND
LOVE
EERLEADERS.

DAVID CARR QUARTERBACK

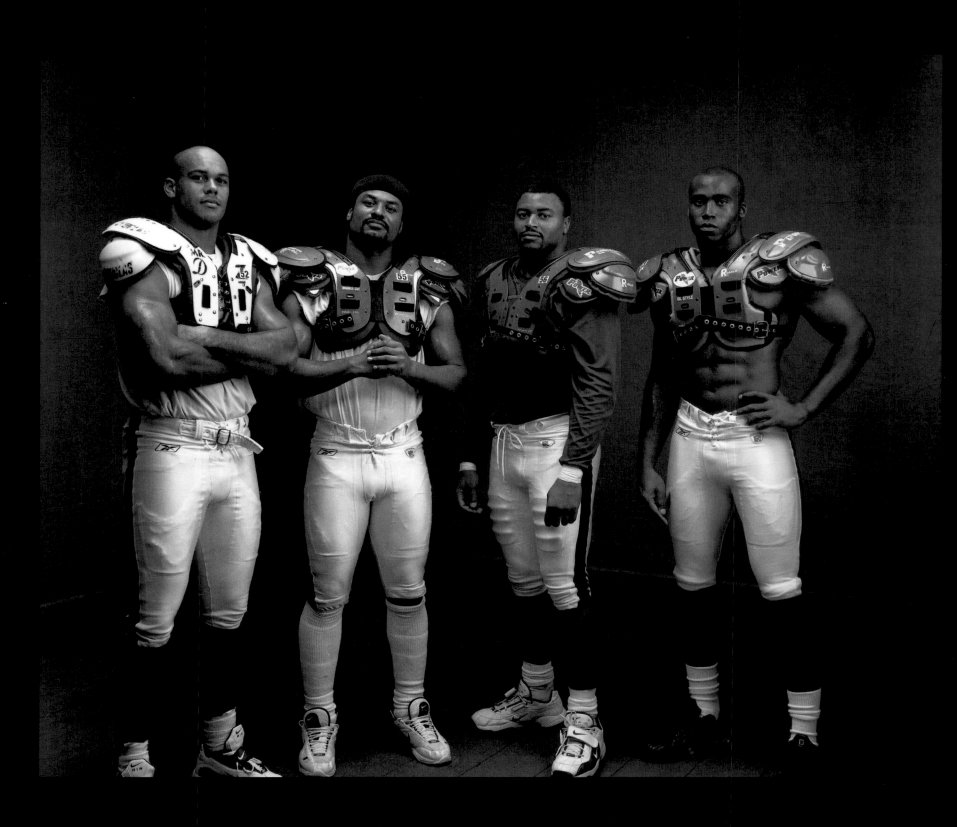

STARTING DEFENSIVE LINE **KAILEE WONG, JAMIE SHARPER, JAY FOREMAN, AND KEITH MITCHELL**

CHEERLEADING TEAM **TEXANS CHEERLEADER COORDINATOR ALTO GARY AND TEXANS CHEERLEADERS JACY, BONNIE, SHARLA, JANA, LINDY, ANGELA, J**

JULIE, SAMANTHA, SHAWNA, TAMMY, BROOKE, AMBER, CARISSA, JANNA, SHANNON ANN, LINDY, REGINA, TIFFANY, ANGELA, AND MARY

TACY, TIFFANY, LYNN, MARY, MICHELLE, JENNIFER, SHAWNETTE, RENEE, CARRIE, JIE, KATHERINE, SARAH, ERICA, JULIE, AND SAMANTHA

DIAGRAM FIRST PLAY VERSUS DALLAS

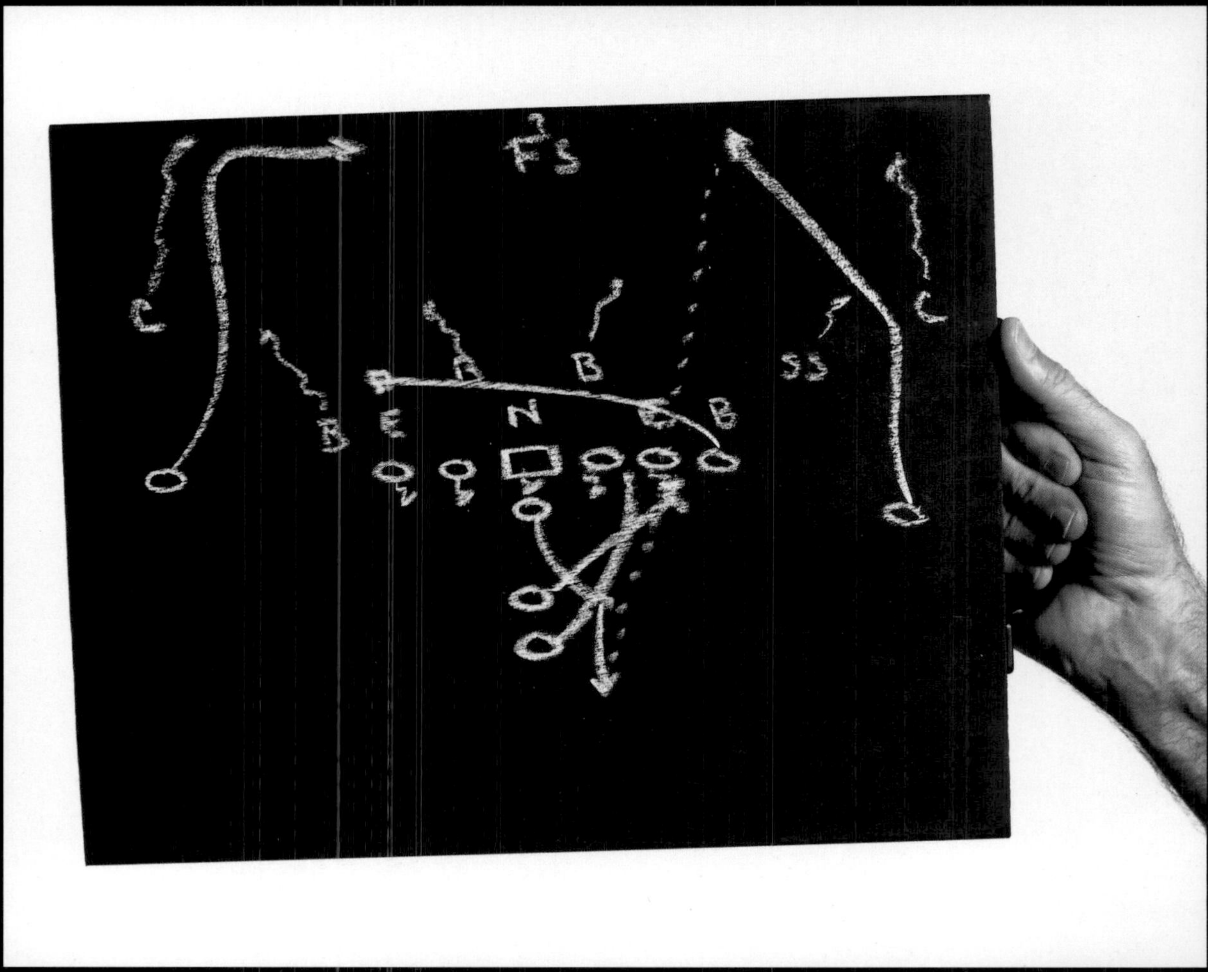

DOM CAPERS HEAD COACH

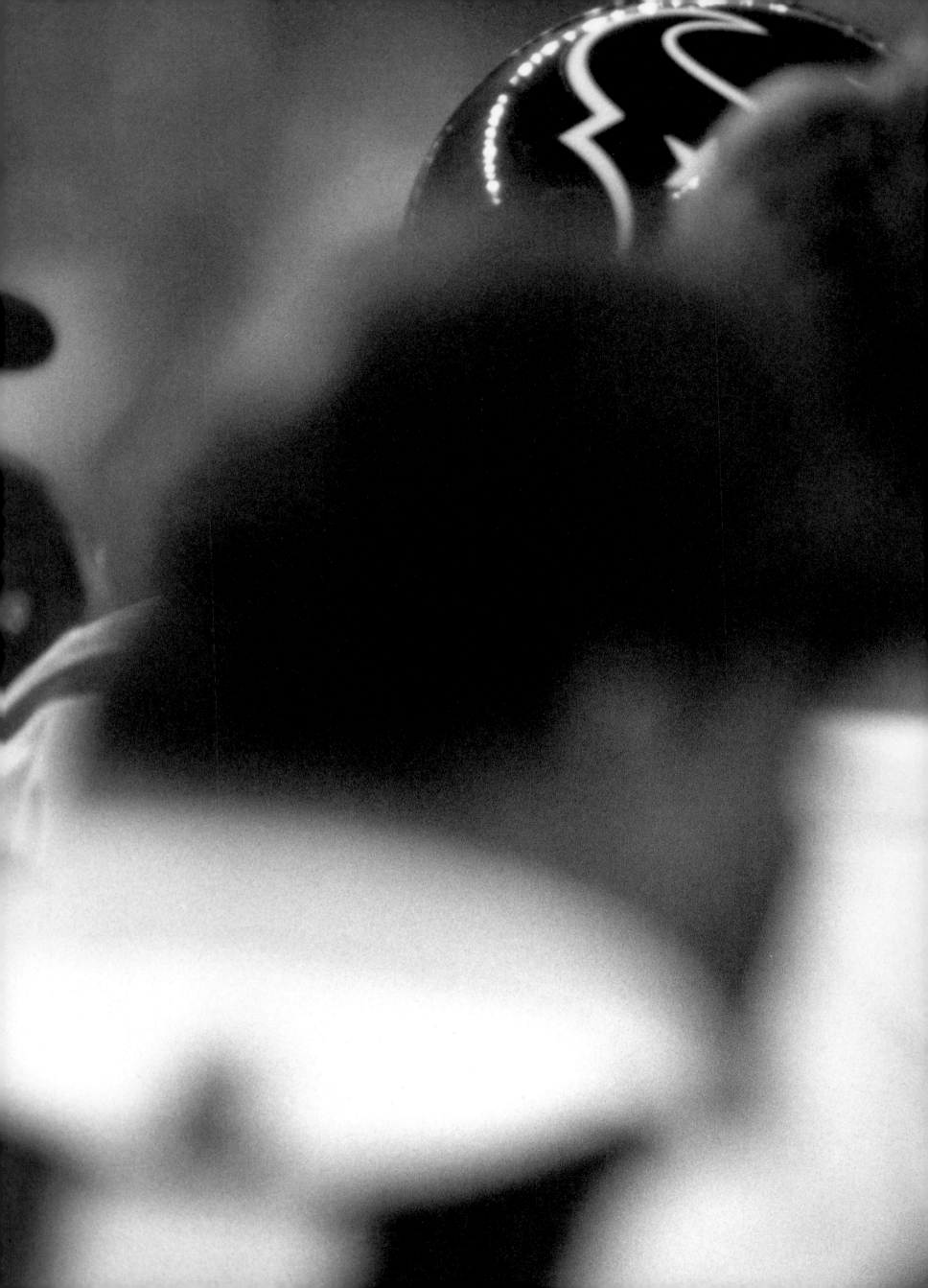

LIKE THE WAY THE CROWD YELLS OUR LAST

NAMES DURING THE INTRODUCTIONS. WE NEED

THE PLACE TO BE NOISY THE WHOLE GAME.
— AARON GLENN. OPENING NIGHT: THE HOUSTON TEXANS' INAUGURAL GAME. 2002

I'm sold on the Texans because of all the disappointments the Oilers gave us for so many years. It's a fresh start, and I wanted to be in it with both feet. I'm never going to turn my back on the Texans.
—HARLON PICKETT, THIRD IN LINE TO ENTER RELIANT STADIUM PARKING LOT FOR TEXANS-COWBOYS GAME. *HOUSTON CHRONICLE*, SEPTEMBER 9, 2002

The Texans logo is a bull's head that looks like a Picasso painting of the Lone Star State.
— GRANT WAHL. *SPORTS ILLUSTRATED*, AUGUST 19, 2002

YOU HATE T

COWBOYS. A

I'VE HATED 'E

ALL MY LIF
— CHRIS LOCKRIDGE, HIS T
FRESH TEXANS TATTOOS
BLAZING ON HIS ARMS. *SPC
ILLUSTRATED*, AUGUST 19, :

I THINK THIS IS THE FIRST TIMI
DOM CAPERS
HAS TAKEN A BREATH IN
TWO YEARS
YOU DON'T ENJOY THIS MOMENT VERY LONG BU
BOY
IT'S A GREAT MOMENT TO HAVI
JOE THEISMANN COMMENTING ON THE AIR AFTER THE WIN OVER DALLAS. OPENING NIGHT: THE HOUSTON TEXANS' INAUGURAL GAME. 2002

...WILL SUPPORT A

...EW TEAM HERE. I

...'ILL PROBABLY BE

...OAMING AT THE

...OUTH WHEN THEY

...TART PLAYING. ME

...ND MY SISTER BOTH.

...en the Oilers
...re here, we
...ldn't do this. This
...one of the best
...ts about football
...ning back to
...uston, being able
...come out here
...ore the game and
...t eat, drink, and
...re fun. It's a little
..., but we have
...nty of beer.

Texas is known for
football. It's a
football state. To
take a team out of a
city was devastating
to the fans—you
could see the look
on people's faces. To
come back to
Houston, where
people know you
already, is like
coming back home.

When the first merchandise comes out, it
will be in my house that same day.

Anyone who doesn't like NFL football is
un-American.

I grew up here and I was an Oilers fan, so
I know what it was like during the great
years. I know this is a big game to the fans
in Houston. The Titans are trying to go to
the Super Bowl. This is our playoff game.
By the time we step on that field, there's
going to be a super-charged atmosphere.

WHEN THE FANS GET EXCITED, PLAYERS GET EXCITED. WHEN I HEAR THAT, I CAN'T WAIT TO GET ON THE FIELD AND HIT SOMEONE.

TWO YEARS AGO, I BOUGHT MY SEASON'S TICKETS, AND I'VE BEEN PAYING FOR THEM OUT OF PAYROLL DEDUCTION EVER SINCE. MY TICKETS ARE IN THE BULLPEN, WHERE THE CRAZY FANS ARE SIT-TING. I'VE MISSED FOOTBALL EVER SINCE THE OILERS LEFT. I STAYED THEIR FAN IN TENNESSEE. BUT NO MORE. I'M A TEXANS FAN NOW.

...ming here, seeing
...reaction of the
...s (gathered at the
...orge Brown
...nvention Center
...the expansion
...ft), then seeing the
...dium, it doesn't get
... better than this.

ANYBODY THAT WOULD PUT UP $700 MILLION TO GET A NEW HOUSTON FOOT-BALL TEAM HAS GOTTA BE A GOOD GUY

PAINTED **TEXANS FAN**

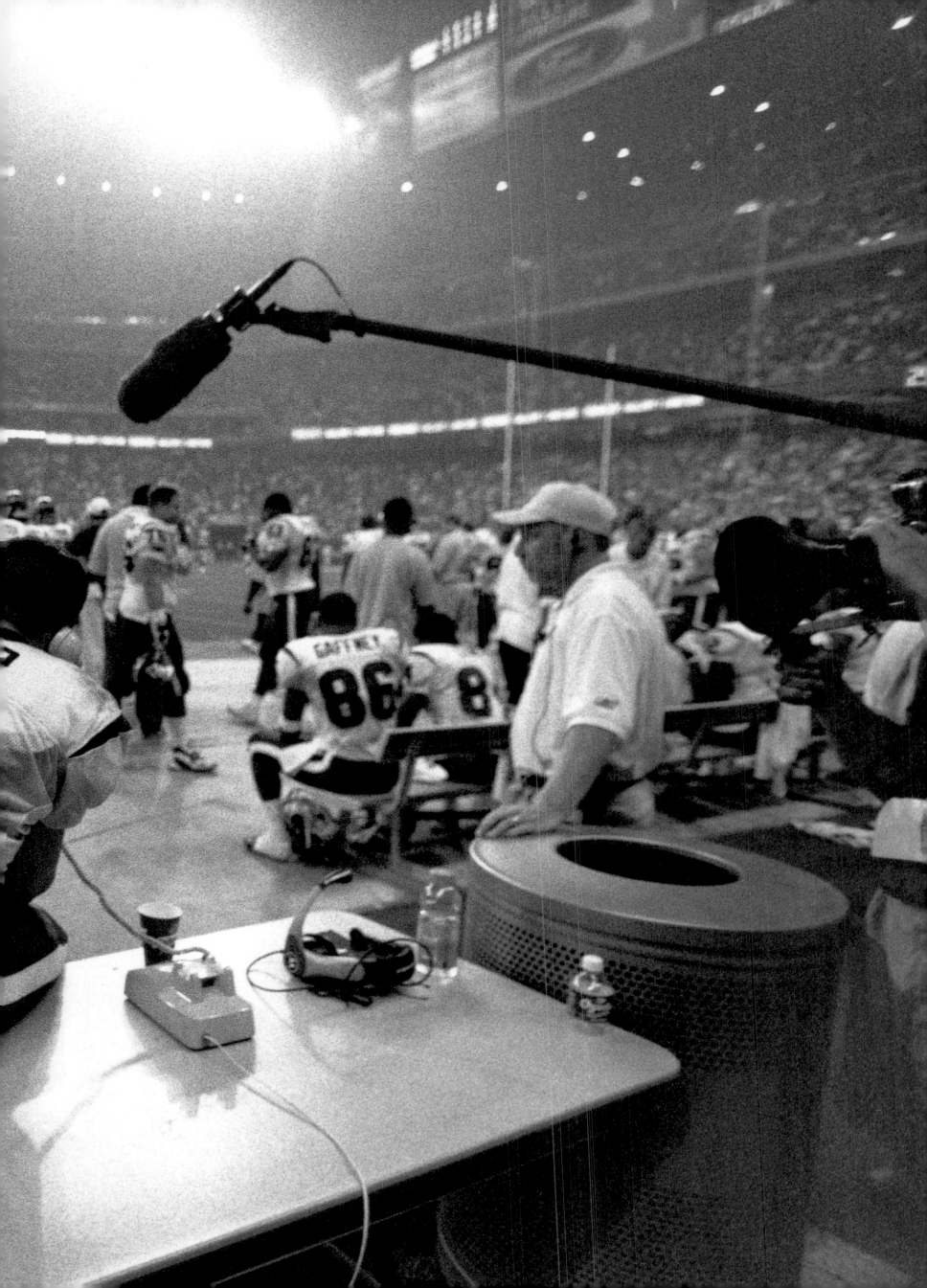

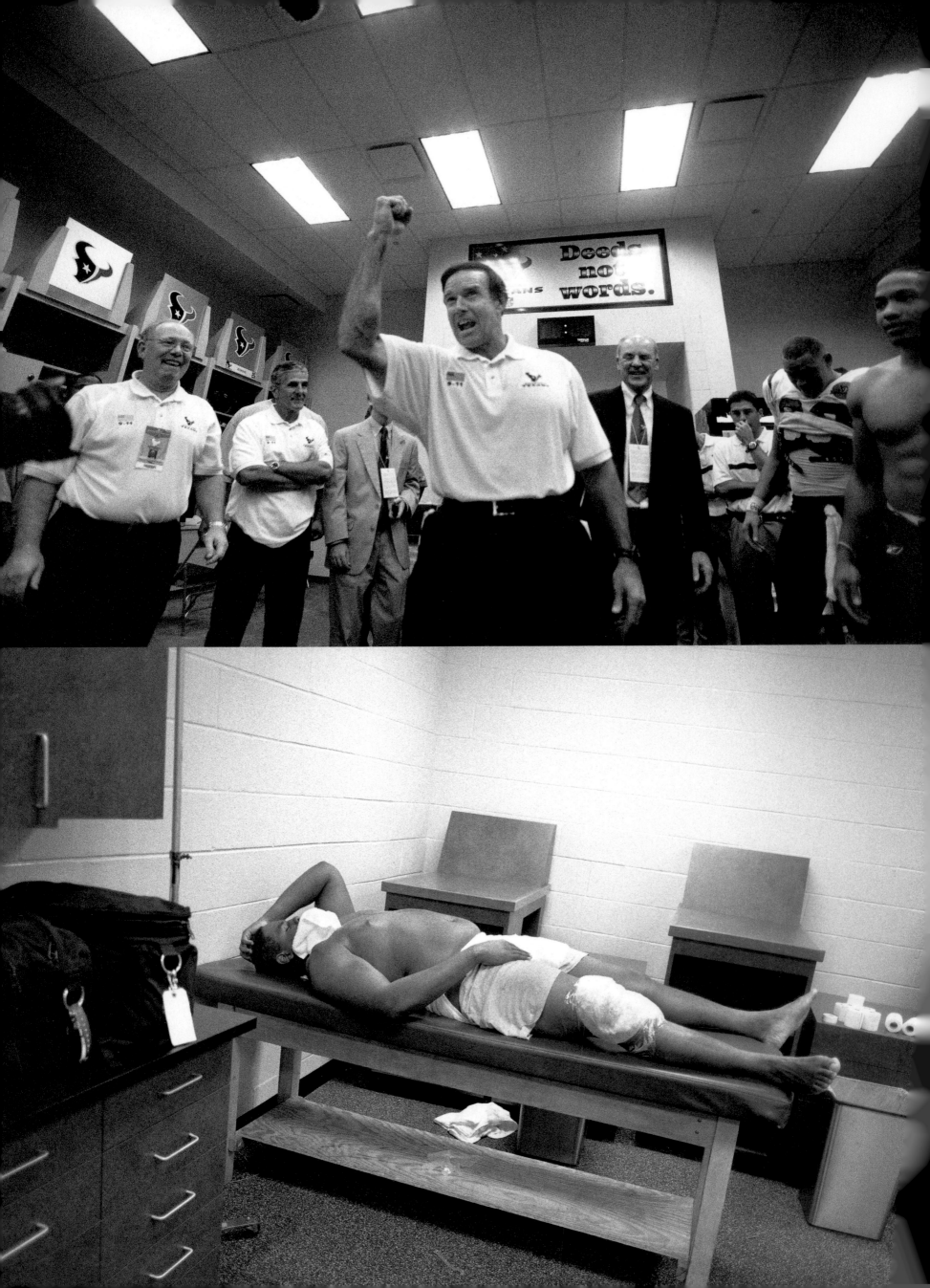

WE DON'T WANT TO BE AMERICA'S TEAM, WE WANT TO BE TEXAS'S TEAM.

—TEXANS OWNER BOB McNAIR. THE SHOWDOWN AGAINST DALLAS. *SPORTS ILLUSTRATED*, AUGUST 19, 2002

"Houston getting the franchise 'underscores what has always been a Houston trait, when the city identifies a goal, it comes together and achieves that goal."
—FORMER HARRIS COUNTY-HOUSTON SPORTS AUTHORITY CHAIRMAN JACK RAINS. "IT'S TOUCHDOWN. . . . HOUSTON." *HOUSTON CHRONICLE*, OCTOBER 7, 1999

IT IS NOT UNTIL YOU'RE REALLY INVOLVED IN THE NFL, THAT YOU REALIZE THAT AN AVERAGE MONDAY NIGHT FOOTBALL GAME IS GOING TO OUTDRAW THE NBA FINALS OR THE MAJOR LEAGUE BASEBALL WORLD SERIES.
—TEXANS SENIOR VICE PRESIDENT STEVE PATTERSON. "HOME GROWN." *HOUSTON CHRONICLE*, OCTOBER 7, 2001

I'm doing it for Houston. If we manage this properly, this can be a tool to bring people together. We have a very diverse community, and this opportunity crosses all lines and ages with a sports team that people have an affinity for.
— TEXANS OWNER BOB McNAIR ON GETTING AN EXPANSION TEAM IN HOUSTON. *NEW YORK TIMES*, APRIL 21, 2002

RULES PREVENT NFL PLAYERS FROM WEARING JEWELRY DURING GAMES. IN PLACE OF HIS WEDDING RING, CARR WEARS A PIECE OF TAPE IN THE SHAPE OF A RING. 'JUST TO LET MY WIFE KNOW I'M STILL THINKING ABOUT HER,' HE SAYS, 'AND THAT SHE'S STILL THERE WITH ME'
"WHAT DRIVES DAVID CARR." *SPORTS ILLUSTRATED*, JANUARY–FEBRUARY 2003

FOOTBALL IS SOMETHING THAT'S IN THE CULTURE HERE. THAT'S WHAT YOU'RE COACHING FOR, YOU WANT TO BE INVOLVED IN SOMETHING THAT'S IMPORTANT TO EVERYBODY AROUND YOU.
—DOM CAPERS. OPENING NIGHT: THE HOUSTON TEXANS' INAUGURAL GAME. 2002

Another thing I like about Bob is that he is a sportsman first and a businessman second.
—INDIANAPOLIS COLTS OWNER JIM IRSAY. "ARE YOU READY FOR SOME FOOTBALL? OWNERS GLAD TO HAVE McNAIR IN THEIR EXCLUSIVE CLUB." *HOUSTON CHRONICLE*, OCTOBER 7, 1999

The one thing I know when we go into a game on Sunday, is you've left no stone unturned and you' done everything yo possibly can to be prepared as you po sibly can be. Becau when the bullets start flying out the on the field, a lot o things can go wror You never know what's going to make the differenc
—DOM CAPERS. "READY AN STEADY." *HOUSTON CHRONIC JANUARY 21, 2001

OTBALL IS A ELIGION

TEXAS, AND THE

HURCH

ROWING EVERY DAY.

ESIDENT STEVE PATTERSON. "FOOTBALL REVIVAL." *HOUSTON CHRONICLE*, APRIL 23, 2001

HERE IS NO OTHER GAME LIKE FOOTBALL. IT'S A GAME

VHERE YOU ALWAYS HAVE TO BE PHYSICALLY AND MENTALLY

TRONG. IN BASEBALL OR BASKETBALL, YOU MIGHT HAVE

AMES BACK-TO-BACK SO IF YOU HAVE A BAD GAME ONE DAY,

OU CAN JUST REDEEM YOURSELF THE NEXT DAY. IN FOOT-

ALL, IF YOU HAVE A BAD GAME ON SUNDAY, YOU HAVE A

VHOLE WEEK TO HEAR ABOUT IT FROM THE MEDIA AND FROM

HE FANS. YOU HAVE TO LOOK AT THAT TAPE WITH THE TEAM.

ND THEN YOU HAVE TO WAIT A WHOLE WEEK TO GET IT BACK.

Houston is the best expansion club in the history of the league. —TITANS GENERAL MANAGER FLOYD REESE ON THE TEXANS. *ESPN.COM*, MAY 30, 2002

The unique thing about sports is it builds camaraderie. Some of my old-time, best friends are guys I played ball with. You don't have that kind of camaraderie in regular business. —TEXANS OWNER BOB MCNAIR. *NEW YORK TIMES*,

I AM VERY IMPRESSED

WITH HOW THIS ORGANI

ZATION HAS BEEN PU

TOGETHER FROM TOP TO

BOTTOM. I DON'T KNOW

HOW IT COULD HAVE

BEEN DONE ANY BETTER. —GIL BRANDT OF NFL.COM. *HOUSTON CHRONICLE*,

HOUSTON'S PRO FOOTBALL HISTORY

COMPILED BY ANNE WILKES TUCKER AND MARISA SANCHEZ
WITH THE HOUSTON TEXANS STAFF

AUGUST 14, 1959
Oilman K.S. "Bud" Adams, Jr., creates the Houston Oilers, a charter member of the American Football League (AFL).

1960
At age 23 Robert McNair, with his wife Janice and their two children, moves from North Carolina to Houston. The son of working-class parents, McNair was the first in his immediate family to graduate from college. With a $3,000 loan, he starts an auto-leasing business.

When Oilers play their first game in 1960, Robert McNair is one of the season ticket holders in Jeppesen Stadium (now Robertson Stadium at the University of Houston). A lifelong sports fan, McNair played football, basketball, and baseball in high school and freshman basketball at the University of South Carolina.

SEPTEMBER 11, 1960
Oilers beat Oakland Raiders 37–22 in their first game.

JANUARY 1, 1961
Oilers win inaugural AFL championship over the Los Angeles Chargers at Jeppesen Stadium. Oilers repeat as AFL champions next season, again over the Chargers.

SEPTEMBER 9, 1968
Oilers move into Houston Astrodome and play first indoor regular-season professional football game in the NFL in a domed stadium. The Kansas City Chiefs beat the Oilers 26-21 before 45,083 fans.

1970
AFL merges with National Football League (NFL), creating the American Football Conference (AFC) and the National Football Conference (NFC) within the NFL. Oilers are 9-45-2 in next four seasons.

1974
The Houston Texans, a World Football League team, play less than a full season at the Astrodome before moving to Shreveport, Louisiana, and becoming the Steamers. That team plays five games in the Astrodome in 1974.

JANUARY 13, 1974
Houston hosts Super Bowl VIII at Rice Stadium, Rice University.

JANUARY 25, 1975
Oilers promote defensive coordinator O. A. "Bum" Phillips to head coach, the 10th coach in 16 seasons. Oilers are 10–4 in Phillips's first season and 55–35 over next six seasons.

APRIL 24, 1978
Oilers draft Heisman Trophy winner Earl Campbell, who becomes national phenomenon when he scores four touchdowns against Miami Dolphins on ABC-TV's "Monday Night Football" broadcast. Campbell is NFL rushing champion and Player of the Year, and he is voted Most Valuable Player for three consecutive years. "Luv Ya Blue" era of Oilers begins.

JANUARY 7, 1979
Pittsburgh Steelers defeat Oilers 34–5 for American Conference Championship.

JANUARY 6, 1980
Oilers lose second AFC title match against Steelers, 27–13.

DECEMBER 31, 1981
Bud Adams fires Bum Phillips after Oilers lose wild-card playoff game against Oakland Raiders, 27–7.

1982
Bob and Janice McNair begin their support of the Museum of Fine Arts, Houston, one of many Houston institutions that benefits from the McNairs' philanthropy and civic commitments. Through their support of a diverse array of charitable, scientific, literary, educational, and religious organizations, the McNairs strive to give back to the community that has meant so much to them.

JUNE 9, 1983
Houston Gamblers, an expansion team of the year-old U.S. Football League, sign University of Miami star quarterback Jim Kelly. He leads Gamblers to a 23-13 record in their two seasons before league folds.

Coached by Jack Pardee, Gamblers averaged 28,152 fans in 1984 when they went 13–5.

1987–1993
Oilers are only team to make playoffs every year from 1987 to 1993, but they never advance beyond the divisional round. In the 1993 wild-card playoff game against the Buffalo Bills, Oilers lose in overtime 41–38, having led 35–3 early in third quarter. One year later, Oilers blow a lead against the Kansas City Chiefs in the fourth quarter and lose 28-20.

AUGUST 11, 1995
Oilers win only 17 games in last three seasons in Houston, and fan attendance drops to fewer than 32,000 a game. Bud Adams, frustrated by the refusal of Houston and Harris County officials to consider using public money to build a replacement for the Astrodome, makes first trip to Nashville to discuss moving Oilers there.

DECEMBER 15, 1996
Only 15,131 fans attend Oilers' final home game in Houston, a 21–13 loss to Cincinnati Bengals.

FEBRUARY 26, 1997
Settlement between Harris County commissioners and Oilers enables team to move immediately to Nashville. In July, city and Astrodome officials approve the deal.

MAY 6, 1997
Bob McNair tells Houston and Harris County officials a stadium plan must be put in place quickly to begin wooing NFL owners.

MAY 1997
Texas legislature approves a bill to create the Houston Sports Authority, which will collect hotel, motel, and car-rental taxes slated for designing, constructing, and equipping a new stadium.

JUNE 18, 1997
After having been denied approval for a National Hockey League expansion

team, Bob McNair turns his interest toward securing a National Football League franchise for Houston.

SEPTEMBER 1997
Steve Patterson, now Senior Vice President and Chief Development Officer of the Houston Texans, joins McNair in his efforts to bring the NFL to Houston.

OCTOBER 17, 1997
Houston Livestock Show and Rodeo officials state that instead of renovating the Astrodome, they will push for building a domed stadium that the Rodeo will share with an NFL team. This is Rodeo's first public statement supporting McNair's efforts.

1998
McNair forms Houston NFL Holdings.

MARCH 23, 1998
The NFL Expansion Committee awards an expansion team to Cleveland. NFL commissioner Paul Tagliabue meets for first time with McNair and Houston and Harris County officials.

MAY 7, 1998
Los Angeles enters bidding for franchise.

FEBRUARY 1999
Bob McNair sells Cogen Technologies, which was the largest privately owned cogeneration company in the world. McNair had founded the company in 1985, and he sold it partly to pursue his dream of owning a pro football team.

FEBRUARY 16, 1999
NFL Expansion Committee meets but does not, as previously promised, pick a winning bidder from the two finalists: Houston and Los Angeles.

MARCH 16, 1999
NFL Expansion Committee gives Los Angeles until September 15 to work out a feasible stadium and ownership plan. If L.A. cannot put a plan together, the committee will then recommend Houston for the 32nd franchise.

OCTOBER 6, 1999
In the end, McNair's enthusiasm, persistence, business acumen, financial portfolio, and partnership with Houston's prominent civic leaders proves overwhelming. National Football League owners vote 29-0 to award franchise to Houston. Bob McNair commits to a record purchase price of $700 million. When asked about the difference between running Cogen Technologies and running a football team, McNair responded, "Maybe 400 people, including our employees, care about Cogen whereas 4 million people care about what happens to the football team."

OCTOBER 14, 1999
Party on the Plaza in Houston honors former Oilers, inviting "Bum" Phillips, Ray Childress, Earl Campbell, and other Oilers to share the stage.

NOVEMBER 29, 1999
Philip Burguières joins the Texans as Vice Chairman.

JANUARY 19, 2000
Texans hire Charley Casserly as Executive Vice President and General Manager of football operations. During his 23 years with the Washington Redskins, Casserly helped mold four Super Bowl teams and won three Super Bowls. Casserly quickly puts together his scouting staff.

MARCH 9, 2000
City, county, and NFL officials break ground on a $367-million football stadium. Houston Livestock Show and Rodeo will be a co-tenant in the stadium and will finance $35 million of the costs. The Texans provide $85 million and public funds will contribute $250 million. The new 69,500-seat stadium will be located next to the Astrodome and will feature the first retractable roof in the NFL. The stadium will also include a 10,000-square-foot weight room (the largest in the NFL), an indoor pool, the largest indoor field in North America, and a 60-yard-long locker room equipped with

shoe dryers for each player. Across the street, three grass practice fields, an indoor practice field with Field Turf, and two buildings for offices and maintenance purposes will sit on 14 acres.

MARCH 25, 2000
The Museum of Fine Arts, Houston, opens the Audrey Jones Beck Building. Gallery 220, which houses 19th-century paintings and sculpture, is named the Janice and Robert C. McNair Gallery in recognition of the McNairs' generous gift to the MFAH.

SEPTEMBER 2000
Infinity Broadcasting Corporation signs a 10-year agreement for exclusive rights to the radio broadcasts of all Texans football games.

SEPTEMBER 6, 2000
After months of research working with focus groups in Houston and throughout Texas, McNair unveils new team's name, logo, and colors at an event in downtown Houston attended by 15,000 fans. The ceremony is televised live on ESPN2, and there are simultaneous unveilings in Austin and San Antonio. For the first time, Texans begin selling season tickets and merchandise on the Internet. At its peak on this Wednesday night, Texans site gets 2,000 hits a second. Eventually Texans sell 59,000 season tickets, 11,000 more than the Oilers sold at their peak.

SEPTEMBER 7, 2000
Texans honored by the Texas Sports Hall of Fame in Waco. The Hall of Fame becomes official archives for Houston's new team.

OCTOBER 26, 2000
Reliant Energy acquires the naming rights for new stadium and convention complex previously known as Astrodomain Complex. The 32-year agreement to acquire the naming rights for five different buildings and the complex is the most comprehensive naming rights agreement in sports history.

NOVEMBER 1, 2000
NFL announces that Reliant Stadium will host Super Bowl XXXVIII on February 1, 2004.

JANUARY 21, 2001
Texans hire Dom Capers as head coach. Capers served as the defensive coordinator for the Jacksonville Jaguars during the 1999 and 2000 seasons. Previously he spent four seasons as head coach of the Carolina Panthers, leading them to a divisional championship in only their second year. His first year finish of 7–9 set an NFL record for most victories by an expansion team. Capers was twice named Coach of the Year.

FEBRUARY 2, 2001
Texans hire Chris Palmer as offensive coordinator. Palmer spent the previous two seasons as head coach of the expansion Cleveland Browns.

APRIL 21, 2001
Texans announce their team mascot, TORO. "Mascots are an important outreach element," says Jamey Rootes, Vice President of Sales and Marketing for the Texans. "Combined with cheerleaders, they bring a softer side to professional sports. It allows us to reach beyond the core football audience and to create a direct connection with the youth. The mascot gives us another way to get into the community and complements our players' public appearances."

MAY 22, 2001
The NFL formally unveils its realignment plan, which features eight four-team divisions. Texans are placed in the AFC South with Indianapolis Colts, Jacksonville Jaguars, and Tennessee Titans, and will play each of these teams twice during the season, once away and once at home.

APRIL 2001
Texans break ground on state-of-the-art training facility.

AUGUST 2001
Bob McNair and Peter Marzio, Director of the Museum of Fine Arts, Houston, discuss their idea of photographing Texans' first year. No NFL team has ever been documented in this way. Their discussion will result in the MFAH book and exhibition based on never-before-seen photographs of the Houston Texans.

AUGUST 18, 2001
Texans cheerleader tryouts are held. From a pool of 1,600 applicants, 35 make the cut. In addition to attending cheerleading practices three times a week and performing at all Texans home games, cheerleaders participate in community programs.

SEPTEMBER 25, 2001
Texans unveil their team uniforms before a crowd of 12,000 fans. Texans cheerleaders also make their debut.

DECEMBER 29, 2001
Texans sign their first 10 players; all are "street" free agents with NFL experience, two of whom are among the team's 56-man opening-day roster.

JANUARY 2002
Texans and the Museum of Fine Arts, Houston, commission photographer Robert Clark and graphic designer/creative director DJ Stout, a partner of Pentagram Design, to work on the book and exhibition *First Down Houston: The Birth of an NFL Franchise.*

JANUARY 14, 2002
Texans hire former Indianapolis Colts defensive coordinator Vic Fangio as their first defensive coordinator.

FEBRUARY 18, 2002
Texans pick 19 players in the NFL expansion draft; seven make the starting team. Draft held at the George R. Brown Convention Center in Houston and televised live on ESPN. "The atmosphere was just unbelievable," said T. Ryan Young on being selected second in the expansion draft. "When I was drafted by the Jets back in 1999, I was booed. To come out to a crowd like that [in Houston] was nice. That will be something I will never forget."

APRIL 20–21, 2002
Texans pick Fresno State quarterback David Carr as their first choice in 2002 NFL Draft. Texans receive 12 selections in the college draft—an NFL record— and 10 of these are on the active roster, with 7 starters during the 2002 season. In building the team, Executive Vice President and General Manager Charley Casserly and Coach Dom Capers focus on young players who can help the team in the future. As a result, only one player on the active roster is over 30, the lowest number in the NFL. The average age of Texans players is 25.6, the fifth youngest in the NFL. The oldest player, Aaron Glenn, is also the most experienced with nine seasons in the NFL. More than 10,000 fans come to Reliant Astrodome to watch the live broadcast of the draft and to participate in activities starting with a 5K race.

APRIL 26, 2002
Texans open their first mini-camp with 99 players, including 25 rookies.

JULY 22, 2002
Standing-room-only crowds of 1,500 fans watch a practice session, the first of eight evening sessions open for fans to watch during training camp. Tickets are required, but are free. The tickets were gone within hours of becoming available on July 13.

AUGUST 2, 2002
Preseason begins with 27,536 fans watching a scrimmage against the Dallas Cowboys at University of Houston's Robertson Stadium.

AUGUST 5, 2002
Texans make their preseason debut in the Pro Football Hall of Fame Game in Canton, Ohio, on "Monday Night Football." New York Giants defeat Texans 34–17.

AUGUST 10, 2002
Texans defeat New Orleans Saints in New Orleans, 13–10.

AUGUST 17
Texans lose to Kansas City Chiefs in Kansas City, 19–9.

AUGUST 24, 2002
Reliant Stadium opens with Texans playing preseason game against Miami Dolphins. Texans lose 24–3. Fans welcome tailgating opportunities, which were not allowed in Astrodome parking lot. Despite the August heat, fans arrive four hours before game time to set up their barbecue pits (ranging from state-of-the-art to homemade).

AUGUST 30, 2002
Texans play second game in Reliant Stadium against Tampa Bay, resulting in a 17–13 loss.

SEPTEMBER 8, 2002
Fans begin lining up hours before gates to parking lots at Reliant Stadium open for the first game of Texans' first season. Texans defeat Dallas Cowboys 19–10 and become only the second expansion team to win their first game. Texans are also only the second expansion team to score on their first possession of the football. Capers is selected as Staples NFL Coach of the Week. Veteran center Steve McKinney said, "This is the most exciting victory I've ever been a part of. This is an awesome feeling." Running back Jonathan Wells said, "We don't play those guys for another four years. We're going to hold the crown until we see them again." Charley Casserly reminds listeners that this is a historic moment because no expansion team has won its first game in 41 years. "It's a lot harder to do it today than it was back in 1961," he said. "The last team that tried this lost 43–0 and that was only three years ago."

SEPTEMBER 15, 2002
After thrilling first victory, Texans return to earth at Qualcomm Stadium, where San Diego Chargers defeat them 24–3. "We came out flat," said tight end Billy Miller, "and we just got beat."

SEPTEMBER 22, 2002
Texans lose to Indianapolis Colts at Reliant Stadium, 23–3. "I don't get upset when someone just outright beats us," safety Chris Carter said. "But that didn't happen today and that hurts. When we executed, they didn't make plays. When we didn't execute, they did."

SEPTEMBER 29, 2002
Philadelphia Eagles defeat Texans in Philadelphia, 35–17.

"The result was the same as the last two weeks," wrote *Houston Chronicle* reporter Carlton Thompson, "but it wasn't all doom and gloom for the Texans. David Carr passed for a season-high 188 yards and matched his career-best with two touchdown tosses to Corey Bradford."

Punter Chad Stanley named AFC Special Teams Player of the Month for September.

OCTOBER 13, 2002
Buffalo Bills defeat Texans at Reliant Stadium, 31–24. Texans never trail until Bills score with 3:55 remaining in the game. "You go out there and fight your butt off, and it hurts to lose like this," Texans cornerback Marcus Coleman said. "What hurts the most is that we had the game won. We're still our own worst enemy." Texans are penalized 11 times. Offensively the team establishes new highs for points, first downs, and passing and rushing yards.

OCTOBER 20, 2002
Cleveland Browns defeat Texans in Cleveland, 34–17. Texans outgain Cleveland by 124 yards and play their best game, statistically, to date. But dropped passes, sacks, and penalties once again defeat the Texans. "It's the same thing every time," Texans safety Matt Stevens said. "It's a play here, a play there. We're in the games, but we never play a complete game. We never play for the entire 60 minutes."

OCTOBER 27, 2002
Texans post their first road win in franchise history by defeating the Jacksonville Jaguars, 21–19. Texans trail 9–7 at halftime, but take the lead three times in the second half, the final time on Kris Brown's game-winning field goal with 2:11 remaining. "Steel wool could not have wiped the smiles of the Texans' faces after the victory," reported the *Houston Chronicle.* "We needed a win," said cornerback Aaron Glenn, "and I like the way we won it. We won a close game, and good teams find ways to win close games."

NOVEMBER 3, 2002
Cincinnati Bengals win at Reliant Stadium, 38–3. "They took their belts off, and they whipped us," Texans tight end Billy Miller said. "They could have been reported to Child Protective Services. If we were businessmen, we might have been fired." The defense, which had held opponents to fewer than 300 yards in four of the previous seven games, surrenders 390 yards to Bengals offense.

NOVEMBER 10, 2002
Tennessee Titans defeat Texans in Nashville, 17–10. Texans defense holds Titans to 251 yards, but offense has its worst game since week 3. Texans threaten late in the fourth quarter. "Any time you put yourself in a position to

at least tie it up at the end of the game, you made enough plays to get you there [but] just not enough to overcome the things you did wrong," said Texans receiver JaJuan Dawson.

NOVEMBER 15, 2002
Ultimate Fan contest at Reliant Stadium selects George Lazaneo, Texan Elvis, and five finalists who are presented at the Texans–Giants game.

NOVEMBER 17, 2002
Jacksonville Jaguars defeat Texans at Reliant Stadium, 24–21. Jaguars build a 24–7 lead, but two 4th-quarter touchdown runs by David Carr pull Texans to within three points with 2:04 remaining in the game. "Things just didn't turn out the way we wanted on that last drive," said right guard Fred Weary. "Eventually we're going to get things on the right track. Fortunately, the fans are still behind us."

NOVEMBER 24, 2002
Texans post third victory with 16–14 defeat of the New York Giants at Reliant Stadium. Texans kicker Kris Brown boots a 50-yard field goal with 6:57 remaining, and Texans defense turns Giants away on their final three drives to preserve another win. "That's life in the NFL," said Texans coach Dom Capers. "Hang in there, keep fighting, and find a way to win."

DECEMBER 1, 2002
Indianapolis Colts defeat Texans in Indianapolis, 19–3. In the first 6½ minutes of the game, Colts turn two Texans turnovers into 10 points and lead throughout the remainder of the game. Texans, who enter this game as the second-most penalized team in the NFL, receive 14 penalties, a season high. "We just keep digging ourselves in these holes," Texans defensive end Gary Walker said. "It's happened to us several times this year and it's hard to keep trying to dig out of it." Texans defense holds Colts to 278 yards instead of the 351 yards per game that Colts had averaged.

DECEMBER 8, 2002
Texans defeat Pittsburgh Steelers in Pittsburgh, 24–6. Cornerbacks Aaron Glenn and Kenny Wright return three Steelers' turnovers for touchdowns. Glenn scores on two interception returns of 70 and 65 yards, while the offense manages only 47 yards, an NFL record for fewest yards by a game-winning team. "We would have been better off staying on the bus," quarterback David Carr said of the Texans' offense. The stunned Steelers had won six of their last eight games before this one. Aaron Glenn named AFC Defensive Player of the Week.

Win against Steelers makes Texans the first expansion team to win a game in each month of NFL regular season.

DECEMBER 15, 2002
Baltimore Ravens win at Reliant Stadium, 23–19. Nine penalties, dropped passes, and turnovers mar a game that the Texans had a chance to win on their last offensive possession. "We can't expect to go out and have those types of errors and expect to win a football game," said coach Capers. "There is a fine line between winning and losing." It is the fourth game that Texans lose by seven points or less. Avion Black named AFC Special Team Player of the Week.

DECEMBER 22, 2002
Washington Redskins defeat Texans at FedEx Field, 26–10. Texans allow opponent a season-high 437 yards. With 10 penalties, Texans reach double figures for the sixth time and allow three sacks. Texans offense does not score a touchdown for the third time in its last four games. "Every loss in this business is tough to take," said cornerback Marcus Coleman, "but we played pretty poorly in this one."

DECEMBER 29, 2002
A stadium-record crowd of 70,694 turns out to see Texans' season finale against Tennessee Titans. The AFC South Champion Titans win 13–3.

Texans end their first season 4-12, tying the record for second-most wins by an expansion team. Quarterback David Carr was one of three NFL quarterbacks to take every snap. During the season, Carr was sacked 76 times, a single-season NFL record. Texans played eight games against playoff teams, winning two. Their two road wins tied them with Carolina Panthers, Jacksonville Jaguars, and Cleveland Browns for the most victories by an expansion team.

During the season, Punter Chad Stanley led the NFL with 34 fair catches and 36 punts inside the 20-yard line. His total of 114 punts tied the NFL record for most punts in a season.

More than one million fans saw the Texans play in their first season; the Texans played before sold-out crowds for all eight home games. The Texans were the most-watched television show in Houston 12 of the 16 weeks of their first season. In week one, the Texans–Cowboys game televised on ESPN was the third highest rated show in ESPN history.

JANUARY 2003
Cornerback Aaron Glenn and defensive end Gary Walker are Pro Bowl starters, marking first time since AFL-NFL merger in 1970 that a first-year expansion team is represented at the Pro Bowl.

APRIL 26, 2003
Texans begin second year by selecting University of Miami wide receiver Andre Johnson in the first round of the 2003 draft. Johnson is one of 10 draft picks.

ACKNOWLEDGMENTS
BY ANNE WILKES TUCKER

"PEOPLE ASK ME IF BOB AND JANICE MCNAIR ARE TOO GOOD to be true," said John Adger, bloodstock manager at the McNairs' Stonerside Stable. "I tell them they are just what they appear to be. They are really good people."

This quote epitomizes the entire Texans organization. Mr. McNair has hired those whom he regards not only as talented professionals, but also as really good people. I would like to thank Mr. and Mrs. McNair for giving the Museum of Fine Arts, Houston, the opportunity to produce the photography exhibition and book *First Down Houston: The Birth of an NFL Franchise*. I also want to acknowledge the members of the Texans staff who worked with the MFAH staff throughout the year: James C. Rootes, Senior Vice President and Chief Sales and Marketing Officer; David Peart, Vice President of Corporate Sales; Kim Babiak, Director of Marketing; and Carter Toole, Director of Internet Services and Publications. Thanks go also to Carl Bassewitz of The Bassewitz Group for sharing his expertise in sports publishing.

During the year of photographing the Texans and then producing the book and organizing the exhibition, we worked particularly closely with Tony Wyllie, Vice President-Communications for the Texans, to make all the necessary appointments with various members of the organization and to secure permissions. We are indebted to Kevin Cooper, Media Relations Assistant, for assisting us with research and fact checking. Coach Dom Capers, his staff, and all the team players were very generous with their time working with Robert Clark. Without their cooperation and support, we would not have this book.

Robert Clark was our first choice as the project photographer for *First Down Houston*, and he delivered all that we had hoped to achieve. Sports photography offers few "second chances." A good photographer anticipates the best shots before they happen and carefully places himself to gain the best perspective for each picture.

The Board of Trustees of the Museum of Fine Arts, Houston, of which Robert McNair is a member, are essential to the success of every project at the MFAH. Mr. and Mrs. McNair have been patrons of the museum for over two decades. Director Peter C. Marzio, who conceived this project with Mr. McNair, offered wise advice throughout. We thank Siemens for its support of the exhibition.

I would also like to thank the museum staff who have worked on behalf of the exhibition and book, particularly Diane Lovejoy, publications; Jack Eby and Bill Cochrane, design; Gwen Goffe, administration; Karen Vetter, exhibitions; Margaret Mims, education; Phenon Finley-Smiley, graphics; and Marty Stein, photographic services. Annalisa Palmieri and Marisa Sanchez in the photography department, as well as summer intern Emily Gerger, each contributed enormously to the project. Ms. Palmieri worked with Robert Clark to coordinate all travel and logistical aspects. Ms. Sanchez worked with me on the research and writing of the book.

From the beginning, DJ Stout of Pentagram Design helped to shape the project through his discussions with Robert Clark and me. With his able associate Erin Mayes, DJ worked with me to edit the 1,100 contact sheets down to the 225 photographs reproduced in the book; of these, 86 were selected for the exhibition. We thank DJ and Erin for the handsome design of this book.

The MFAH has a fine collection of sports photographs, and we thank Mr. and Mrs. McNair and the Houston Texans for giving the museum the photographs commissioned for *First Down Houston*. These works make a rich addition to our holdings.

ANNE WILKES TUCKER
The Gus and Lyndall Wortham Curator of Photography,
The Museum of Fine Arts, Houston

ACKNOWLEDGMENTS
BY ROBERT CLARK

FIRST, I WOULD LIKE TO THANK THE PEOPLE WHO HIRED me for *First Down Houston: The Birth of an NFL Franchise:* Anne Wilkes Tucker, Peter Marzio, and the Board of Trustees of the Museum of Fine Arts, Houston. I hope that people who view this work will see the beauty in athletic grace as well as the community that can be created by a professional team.

To Anne, thank you for the opportunity and your guidance. To Peter, thank you for your leadership and for conceiving this project with Robert McNair.

I thank Robert and Janice McNair for their belief in the project and for bringing football back to a city that truly loves the game.

My thanks to Siemens for supporting this exhibition.

The Texans players, coaches, and staff always made me feel welcome. Of them, two folks were of special help: Tony Wyllie and Kevin Cooper. Tony was always interested in the success of this project, even if he didn't understand the reason that "I wanted to shoot something the way I wanted to." Tony did all he could to help, and he navigated between the coach and the players and me so that I could tell as truthful a story as possible. Kevin Cooper took a personal interest in the project while the first season was under way. His help was invaluable, especially in the editing and fact-finding phases of the project.

Thanks go to DJ Stout and Erin Mayes of Pentagram Design. I am grateful to DJ for his friendship and guidance during the course of this project, as well as for his overall vision of the book. DJ, you recommended me for this job, and I'm not sure I can repay this gift. Erin showed endless good humor and dedicated her considerable design skills to this work. Erin and DJ, you took my work and made it greater than the sum of its parts.

Gregory Heisler, your boundless energy and love of photography was more inspiration than you could imagine. To Walter Iooss, Dan Peak, Bo Rader, John Huba, Chris Johns, Kurt Mutchler, Jose Azel, Chris Anderson, Bert Fox, Bill Cramer, and Tom Kennedy, your work and friendship have inspired me and helped me to understand the value of visual communications.

My thanks to David Coventry, a friend who assisted me both in the technical sense of the word and in the aesthetic direction I pursued. Your help contributed a large part to the success of this project.

To Buzz Bissinger, the brilliant author of *Friday Night Lights*, thank you for the opportunity to work with you on a project in 1988 that changed my life and still affects the work I do today.

I would also like to acknowledge the people from A Small Darkroom: Richard Foulser, Phil South, Rebecca Daly, chief printer Jessica Anderson, and printers Libby McLinn and Kent Larsson. Thank you for your commitment to excellence in both the prints for the book and the exhibition. Thanks are due also to Dave Metz, David Sparer, Steve Losi, and Rudy Winston of Canon Professional Service.

Fotocare has and will always be my No. 1 choice, and I thank its owner Jeff Hersch and rental manager Fred Blake.

Thompson Photo Lab, Houston, must be commended for its great job on developing the film for this project.

At the Museum of Fine Arts, Houston, Annalisa Palmieri took at least one hundred phone calls from me while also keeping track of all the details with Anne and DJ. I'm not sure how she always managed to track people down and keep the information straight. Thank you for your assistance.

I would like to thank my family, who has supported me without fail. To Russ and Dora Lou Clark, my parents, thank you for my upbringing and my education, both of which I can see in the work that I do now. To my brother, Steve, the former sports editor of my home-town newspaper, thanks for the first fifty assignments of my career and for your constant support. To my brothers and sisters, Lynn and Michael Burke, Cindy Maddux, Sara Clark, and Patrick Clark, thanks for always allowing me to talk with you about my work and my goals.

For the warmth of your friendship, my thanks go to the Jew and Geralds families, Marlene and Michael, Ed, Phillip, Danny, Eva and Luca.

Most importantly, I thank Lai Ling Jew. I could not have done this work without your support. You understood that we were trying to do a book about something more important than winning and losing, and you offered unconditional support, along with a creative eye that makes this book part yours. I love you.

ROBERT CLARK
June 6, 2003

CAPTIONS

PHOTOGRAPHS ARE IDENTIFIED CLOCKWISE FROM UPPER LEFT.
ALL PHOTOGRAPHS WERE TAKEN IN 2002 AND WERE GIVEN BY JANICE S. AND ROBERT C. MCNAIR AND THE HOUSTON TEXANS TO THE MUSEUM OF FINE ARTS, HOUSTON.

COVER
Steve McKinney, Center

PLATE 1
Reliant Stadium

PLATE 2
Fans

PLATES 3-6
Fifty-Nine Diner, Houston;
Fans at Hall of Fame Game,
Canton, Ohio, August 5;
First Game Sign, Houston,
September 8; Fifty-Nine Diner
Waiter Wears Jersey Signifying
That Houston Was the 32nd
NFL Franchise, Houston

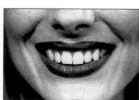

PLATE 7
Smile of Stacy,
Texans Cheerleader

PLATE 8
Wide Receiver Corey Bradford
Attempts to Catch a
Touchdown Pass in a Game
against Jacksonville Jaguars,
Houston, November 17

PLATE 9
Bob McNair's Shoes

PLATE 10
Quarterback David Carr
Meets the Press during
Training Camp

PLATE 11
San Diego Charger Giving
Quarterback David Carr a
Hand, San Diego, September 15

PLATE 12
Fans Reach for a "High Five"
and Autographs

PLATE 13
Training Camp Wind Sprints:
Dwaune Jones, Clif Groce, and
Atnaf Harris

PLATE 14
Head Coach Dom Capers
during Training Camp Practice

PLATES 15-18
Quarterback David Carr Is
Photographed by Bill Frakes
for *Sports Illustrated*; Running
Back James Allen and Other
Players Stretch after Training
Camp Practice; Todd
Grantham, Defensive Line
Coach, and Players in Training
Camp; Coach Jedd Fisch with
Play Flip Chart at Practice

PLATE 19
Offensive Line Drill: Jelani
Hawkins, Jeremy McKinney,
Chris Lorenti, Craig
Heimburger, and Jerry Wisne

PLATES 20-21
Quarterback David Carr and
Offensive Coordinator
Chris Palmer; Wide Receiver
Sherrod Gideon Cools Off

PLATE 22
Linebacker Jason Lamar Cools
Off during Training Camp

PLATES 23-26
Corey Bradford, Wide Receiver;
Tackle Tony Boselli Rehabs His
Shoulder; Players in Heated
Pool; Wide Receiver Jabar
Gaffney Stretches Before Game
with Washington Redskins,
Washington, D.C., December 22

PLATE 27
Defensive Tackle Jerry
Deloach in a Tackling Drill
during Practice

PLATE 28
Practice under the "Bubble"

PLATES 29-32
Player Returning to the Hotel
Room after a Day of Practice
during Training Camp; Flight to
Game with Tennessee Titans,
November 9; Players Before the
Game Playing "Halo" on the
X-Box; Free Safety Kevin
Williams Relaxes Before a Game

PLATES 33-34
Linebacker Keith Mitchell on
the Sidelines; Defensive Player

PLATE 35
Rookie Linebacker Greg
White Heads Home Late after
Training Camp Practice

PLATES 36-39
Reliant Stadium and the
Astrodome; Grounds Crew; Tuba
Practice for Pep Band; Alto Gary,
Cheerleader Coordinator

PLATE 40
Pre-Season Scrimmage at
Robertson Stadium on the
University of Houston
Campus: Texans vs.
Cowboys, August 2

PLATE 41
Fan Views 2002 Inductees,
Hall of Fame Game,
Canton, Ohio, August 5

PLATES 42-43
First Fan into the First Regular
Season Game Gets a Kiss
from His Father, Houston,
September 8; David Carr Fan
Runs for Refreshments

PLATE 44
Texans Fans Head Home

PLATE 45
Before the Skit in
Kansas City, August 17

PLATE 46
Corey Bradford, Wide Receiver

PLATES 47-48
Jonathan Wells, Running Back

PLATE 49
Kevin Williams, Free Safety

PLATES 50-51
Jason Bell, Cornerback;
Jeff Posey, Linebacker

PLATE 52
Billy Miller's Hand; Phil. 4:13:
"I Can Do All Things Through
Christ Who Strengthens Me"

PLATE 53
Corey Bradford, Wide Receiver

PLATE 54
Gary Walker,
All-Pro Defensive Tackle

PLATE 55
Quarterback David Carr
Stretches Before a Game

PLATES 56-58
David Carr Wraps a "Wedding
Ring" made of Tape Before a
Game; Trainer Tom Colt Applies
Tape Before a Game; Pre-Game
Stretch: Coach Dan Riley Assists
Wide Receiver Frank Murphy

PLATE 59
Running Back James Allen,
Linebacker Jeff Posey, and
Linebacker Troy Evans
Adjust Armor Before A Game

PLATES 60-62
Corey Bradford's Shoulder Pads
and Jersey; Taped Hands;
Coaches' Shoes That Are Packed
Every Week for Game Day

PLATE 63
Rookie Guard Fred Weary
Reads a Bible Before a Game

PLATE 64
Pre-game Thoughts: Head
Coach Dom Capers Before
Road Game with Tennessee
Titans, December 29

PLATES 65-67
Wide Receiver Avion Black
Concentrates Before a Game;
Tight End Billy Miller Prays
Before the Tennessee Titans
Game, Nashville, Tennessee,
November 10; Longsnapper
Sean McDermott Concentrates
Before the Game against the
Washington Redskins, Wash-
ington, D.C., December 22

PLATE 68
Cheerleaders' Shadows

PLATES 69-72
Rookie Quarterback David Carr
prior to a Game; Offensive Coach
Chris Palmer during Halftime;
Offensive Line, Pre-Game at
Kansas City, August 17; Running
Back Moran Norris and fellow
Running Back Jonathan Wells
with Offensive Coordinator
Chris Palmer Mentally Prepare
for Last Game, Houston,
December 29

PLATE 73
Head Coach Dom Capers'
Halftime Speech

PLATE 74
Prayer after Game: Players
Charles Hill and Ryan Young
and Coaches Everett Coleman
and Tony Marciano

PLATES 75-106
Texans Fans

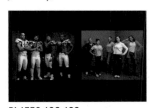

PLATE 107
TV Cameramen Before
Pre-Game Announcements,
Home Game with Baltimore
Ravens, December 15

PLATES 108-111
Head Coach Dom Capers and
the Texans Wait to Enter the
Home Field; Waiting to Enter
Stadium; Head Coach Dom
Capers Checks Time Before the
Kansas City Chiefs Game, Kansas
City, August 17; Dom Capers,
Jerry Deloach, Khari Samuel, Billy
Granville, and Sean McDermott
Listen to the Star-Spangled
Banner at Kansas City, August 17

PLATE 112
Kicker Kris Brown Heads to
the Field, 2002

PLATE 113
Jimmy McClain, Rookie
Linebacker, Pre-Game Entry,
Houston

PLATES 114-117
Running Back James Allen
Responds to Fans; Quarterback
David Carr Responds to Fans;
Quarterback David Carr and
Tight End Kaseem Sinceno
Respond to Fans; Quarterback
David Carr Responds to Fans

PLATES 118-119
Quarterback David Carr Poses
after Practice

PLATES 120-121
Seth Payne, Defensive Tackle;
Jeff Posey, Linebacker

PLATES 122-123
Starting Defensive
Linebackers Kailee Wong,
Jamie Sharper, Jay Foreman,
and Keith Mitchell;
Cheerleaders: Julie, Regina,
Stacy, Jacy, and Carissa

PLATE 124
Houston Texans Owner
Bob McNair

PLATES 125-126
Fred Weary, Guard; Aaron
Glenn, All-Pro Cornerback

PLATE 127
Texans Cheerleaders

PLATES 128-129
Dom Capers, Head Coach;
Diagram of First Play versus
Dallas

PLATE 130
Defensive Tackle Gary Walker
Takes the Field

PLATE 131
The "Bull Pen," Houston

PLATES 132-135
Fans Reach Out to Players;
Punter Chad Stanley Warms Up
in Kansas City, August 17;
Center Steve McKinney and
Other Players Stretch Before a
Game; Jamie Sharper, Linebacker

PLATE 136
Dallas Cowboys Owner Jerry
Jones and Houston Texans Owner
Bob McNair Share a Moment
prior to the Texans' First Victory,
Houston, September 8

PLATE 137
Center Steve McKinney
Snaps the Ball

PLATE 138
Defensive Tackle Gary Walker and
Fellow Defensive Tackle Jerry
Deloach versus the New York
Giants, Houston, November 24

PLATES 139-140
Home Game; Cheerleaders
Lindy and Carissa with
Enthusiastic Fans

PLATE 141
Wide Receiver Jermaine Lewis
Returns a Punt, with Coverage
from Linebacker Jimmy McClain

PLATES 142-144
Houston Texans Defensive
Line and Jacksonville Jaguars
Offensive Line, Houston,
November 17; Loose Ball;
Texans Defense, Houston,
November 17

PLATE 145
Quarterback David Carr

PLATES 146-149
Quarterback David Carr versus
New York Giants, Houston,
November 24; Quarterback
David Carr Cheers on Defense;
Cornerback Aaron Glenn
Reacts to a Turnover;
Tight End Billy Miller

PLATE 150
Dancing Cheerleaders

PLATES 151-158
Dancing Fan

PLATE 159
Scoreboard Repair prior to the
First Home Game

PLATE 160
Dom Capers, Head Coach

PLATES 161-162
Running Back James Allen
Carries the Ball Gang Tackle:
Linebackers Troy Evans
and Jay Foreman Bring
Down Washington Redskins
Defensive Back Bruce
Branch, Washington, D.C.,
December 22

PLATE 163
David Carr in a Huddle with
Steve McKinney, DeMingo
Graham, Chester Pitts,
and Jabar Gaffney

PLATES 164-165
Texans Elvis George
Lazaneo, 2002 Ultimate
Fan Contest Winner

PLATE 166
Texans Twins:
Jay and Ray Joiner

PLATES 167-168
Fans after Game; Sisters

PLATES 169-170
Barbecue at Tailgate Party;
Barbecue Tailgater

PLATE 171
Tailgate Superman

PLATES 172-173
Sleepy Texans Fan;
Tailgater with Texans Tattoo

PLATES 174-175
Texans Fans, 2002; Texans Fan

PLATE 176
Pre-Game Show Before Home
Game with Baltimore Ravens,
December 15

PLATES 177-178
Defensive Tackle Gary Walker,
Pro Bowl Tackle; Cheerleader

PLATE 179
Quarterback David Carr
Hands Off to Running Back
Jonathan Wells

PLATE 180
Jonathan Wells, Running Back

PLATES 181-182
Gary Walker, Defensive Tackle;
Joey Knapp, Tight End

PLATES 183-184
Quarterback David Carr
Tackled by Tennessee Titan
Donald Mitchell, Nashville,
Tennessee, November 10;
Quarterback David Carr and
Washington Redskins Carl
Powell, December 22

PLATES 185-186
Leomont Evans, Strong Safety;
Washington Redskins Rush
on Quarterback David Carr,
Washington, D.C., December 22

PLATE 187
Defensive Team: Kenny Wright,
Eric Brown, Jamie Sharper,
Keith Mitchell, and Seth Payne

PLATES 188-189
Tight End Billy Miller Reacts
to a Referee's Call; Cornerback
Aaron Glenn Stays Loose on
the Sidelines during a Game

PLATE 190
Fans React

PLATES 191-192
Cheerleader's Pom-pom;
Fan and Cheerleaders:
Lindy, Jie, and Stacy;

PLATE 193
The "Bull Pen" from Behind

PLATE 194
Quarterback David Carr Talks
to Chris Palmer in the Press
Box in between Series

PLATES 195-196
Quarterback David Carr;
Texans Stopped Jaguars
Short of the Goal Line

PLATE 197
General Manager Charley
Casserly and Texans Owner
Bob McNair in Founder's
Suite React to a Big Play

PLATES 198-199
Running Back Jonathan Wells
Celebrates Touchdown
against the New York Giants,
Houston, November 24

PLATE 200
Texans Pride

PLATE 201
Post-Game Prayer: Houston
Texans and Indianapolis Colts,
Houston, September 22

PLATES 202-205
Head Coach Dom Capers and
Houston Texans Owner Bob
McNair with the Team after the
Victory over the Dallas Cowboys,
Houston, September 8;
Linebacker Jamie Sharper
Helps Fellow Linebacker
Kailee Wong Take Off His
Shoulder Pads; Linebacker
Jeff Posey Answers Questions
after the Hall of Fame Pre-
Season Game, Canton, Ohio,
August 5; Defensive Tackle
Jerry Deloach Ices His Knee

PLATE 206
Offensive Tackle Jimmy
Herndon Celebrates Victory
over Dallas Cowboys, the
First Win in Franchise History,
Houston, September 8

PLATE 207
Trash Bin in Texans' Locker
Room 1/2 Hour after the Final
Game, December 29

BACK COVER
Reliant Stadium

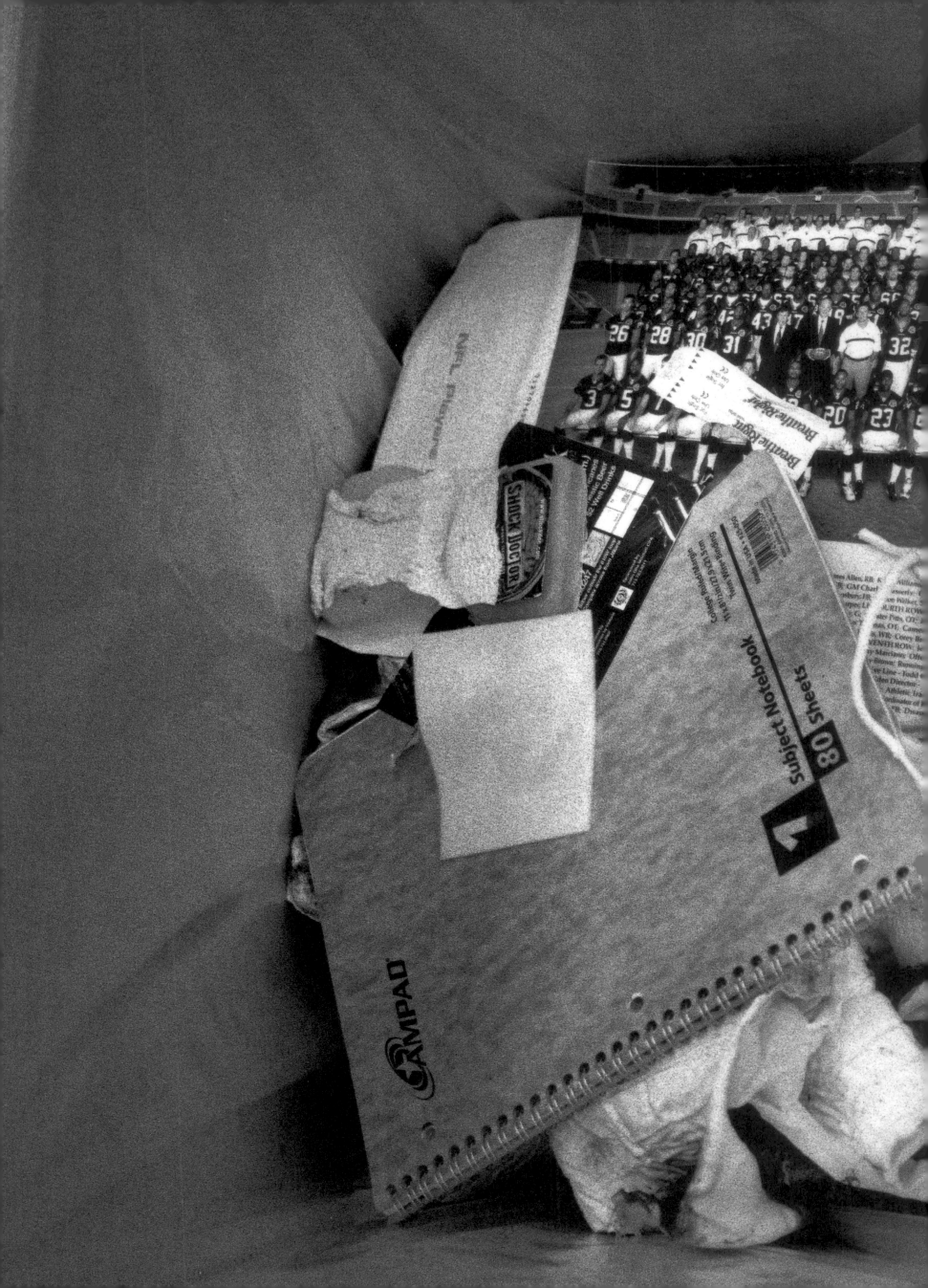